Love & Merry Christmas
to

David Dunlap
from
Aunt Emily
1973

Other aviation books by David C. Cooke

SKY BATTLE: 1914-1918

A British F.E.2 on patrol above a German trench system. These positions were obviously prepared far behind the front lines, to be occupied in the event of retreat.   *U.S. Air Force*

David C. Cooke

SKY BATTLE: 1914-1918

*The Story of Aviation
in World War I*

W · W · NORTON & COMPANY · INC · New York

TO THE OLD GANG—

Herb Powell, Arch Whitehouse, Don Keyhoe,
Joe Archibald, Jesse Davidson, Charles Yerkow,
Fred Lord, Alden McWilliams, Ed Smalle Jr.

Contents

List of Illustrations

Foreword

FOR MANY YEARS I have wanted to write a book about the airplane as a weapon from its earliest struggling days through to the end of World War I. This was the time, as they used to say in the pulp magazines, of iron men and fragile wings. This was the formative period in which aviation as a science was suddenly accelerated.

This book is not meant to glorify combat aviation, for there is nothing glorious in killing or being killed. It is, rather, an attempt to chronicle an era of history honestly and fairly and without national bias, and to assign aviation its proper place in that history.

Most of the air action of the war was only a part of the far more important and enormous struggles which took place on the ground between August 1914 and November 1918. I have tried to show how aviation was employed by both sides in these engagements, listing the failures as well as the successes. However, I have confined myself to the use of the airplane on the Western Front in France, which was the main arena of combat. To have told the story of the airplane in all theatres of operation would have required many more pages than I have here.

This is not another volume dealing primarily with the flying aces, for their stories have been told numerous times, though sometimes with generous slices of legend. As an example, one noted writer quoted the combat log of the *escadrille* to which Georges Guynemer was assigned. The log was quoted exactly, but with one slight alteration. Guynemer was credited with *all* the combats and *all* the victories mentioned in the log for the period, where in actual fact Guynemer was only one of the many pilots involved. The deeds or developments by other men have likewise been magnified in some cases out of all proportion to the truth. I have attempted to correct as many of these old inaccuracies as possible.

Despite my long association with aviation, the task of putting this book together has been formidable. Even the most reliable records and the most trustworthy accounts often seem to contradict each other. The official historians at times slanted material for their own purposes or had only one side of the story, and the airmen who wrote about their experiences generally saw only fragments of any battle. In some cases the airmen involved in a single combat wrote accounts which vary in the sequence of the action as well as the results. I have tried to unravel many of these.

During the years I have collected many bits and pieces of information about World War I aviation—books, letters, diaries, official histories, squadron reports, front-line communiqués. Most of this material was produced by men who helped to write the history of the development of the airplane as a weapon or who were involved in combat. Some of this information has been reprinted in other books, but some of it is new and fresh and virtually unknown.

Now that I have finished my writing job, I hope I have accomplished what I set out to do in the first place. If there are any gaps, these will have to be filled by someone else.

DAVID C. COOKE

"No history can be expected to furnish a full record of all the acts of prowess that were performed in the air during the long course of the war. Many of the best of them can never be known. . . ."
—Sir Walter Alexander Raleigh in *War in the Air*

A Weapon Is Born

Chapter One

A MOMENTOUS EVENT took place in Washington, D.C., on August 1, 1907. There, in a remote office within the gray, foreboding War Department Building in the shadow of the White House, without ceremony and with not even one newspaper reporter present, the Aeronautical Division of the United States Signal Corps was established.

This new division was created by Brigadier General James Allen, the Chief Signal Officer, "to study the flying machine and the possibility of adapting it to military purposes." However, the Aeronautical Divison had not been General Allen's idea. There is no known record of the General's personal beliefs and convictions, but it would not be farfetched to assume that he, along with virtually everyone else in the United States, refused to believe the ridiculous stories that the Wright brothers had actually achieved true flight in a heavier-than-air machine.

The creation of the Aeronautical Division had come down from the highest level of Government—from President Theodore Roosevelt himself. Earlier that year Congressman Herbert Parsons of New York had sent the President clippings from the *Scientific American* magazine, which described the Wright

Flyer and the experiments that the Dayton, Ohio, brothers had undertaken with their machine. Unlike most of the critics, President Roosevelt had an open mind. After all, Alexander Graham Bell had recently demonstrated that the human voice could be sent over a wire, and Thomas Alva Edison had discovered a way to bring electric lights into offices and homes. Why would it not also be possible for men to fly in something other than balloons? The President instructed Secretary of War William Howard Taft to look into the situation, and from Secretary Taft the Executive order filtered down to General Allen.

Captain Charles deForest Chandler, a balloon pilot, was placed in command of the Aeronautical Division. He was also assigned a staff of two enlisted men: Corporal Edward Ward and Private First Class Joseph E. Barrett. Within a few weeks a Cavalry officer and amateur balloon pilot, Lieutenant Frank P. Lahm, became the fourth member of the Division. The previous summer, while in France where he won the first James Gordon Bennett international balloon race starting in Paris, Lieutenant Lahm had listened with extreme interest as Wilbur and Orville Wright talked about their airplane. Convinced that the soft-spoken, unassuming brothers had developed a machine that would have a far-reaching impact on military tactics and strategy, Lahm lost no time in pursuing the matter after he was assigned to the Aeronautical Division.

As a direct result of the interest and efforts of Captain Chandler and Lieutenant Lahm, the Aeronautical Divison, within two months of its founding, submitted a request for two flying machines. The report ended with these words:

> If the United States Army can secure two flying machines which fulfill the requirements of these specifications, military aeronautics in this country will be placed far in advance of the equipment of European armies. This should be worth the cost of $45,000.

After studying this request the War Department, on December 23, 1907, issued detailed specifications for a military airplane. Bids were invited from builders, with a closing date of February 1, 1908.

According to the specifications, the flying machine had to be capable of achieving a speed of 40 miles per hour in still air. The builder selected would be charged a penalty of 10 percent for every mile the plane flew below this speed and would be given a bonus of 10 percent for every mile it flew above the required minimum. The machine also had to be capable of carrying two people with "a combined weight of 350 pounds" and a fuel supply sufficient for a flight of 125 miles. In addition, the specifications insisted that in order to pass acceptance tests, the machine would have to be able to fly nonstop for at least one hour.

Other requirements stipulated, "It is desirable that the flying machine be designed so that it may be quickly and easily assembled, and taken apart and packed for transportation in Army wagons. It should be capable of being assembled in about an hour" and "should be designed as to ascend in any country which may be encountered in field service."

But perhaps the most humorous demands in the specifications, by modern standards, were that the machine should be capable of landing "in a field without requiring a specially prepared spot and without damaging its structure" and that it be so constructed that "it permit an intelligent man to become proficient in its use within a reasonable length of time."

Forty-one replies were received by the War Department to its request for a flying machine. Some of the designs submitted and prices requested were so impossible that it was a wonder the "inventors" even took the trouble to put them on paper. Of the forty-one designers who replied, only Augustus M. Herring and the Wright brothers had had any practical experience with flying machines. The field was quickly narrowed to the Wrights alone, and on February 10, 1908, the Signal Corps signed a contract with the Wright brothers for what was to be the world's first military airplane. The contract stipulated a purchase price of $25,000 and delivery of the completed machine on or before August 28, 1908.

When the Wrights were awarded the contract, they finally had another dream come true. Almost three years previously, on May 28, 1905, Wilbur had written to Octave Chanute, "We stand ready to furnish a practical machine for use in war at once, that is, a machine capable of carrying two men and fuel for a fifty-mile trip." He added, "We have made a formal proposition to the British Government and expect to have a conference with one of its representatives in Dayton very soon." Earlier that year the Wrights had offered their machine to the United States Government and had received a reply from the President of the Board of Ordnance and Fortifications saying they were not interested in "financing experiments." On October 9 the brothers wrote another letter to Washington—this time to the Secretary of War—and again they were turned down.

Just as officials in Washington had treated the Wrights as little more than cranks, so the brothers were considered by the British, the French, and the Germans. The Signal Corps contract was the first true recognition the Wrights had ever received from any official source in any country.

Suddenly, with this contract, new interest was generated in Europe, and in March 1908 the Wrights sold the French Government rights to their flying machine for about $100,000. However, the contract insisted upon two demonstration flights of approximately thirty-one miles, each to be completed within an hour. The contract also insisted that the demonstration flights be made before the end of October.

From December 17, 1903, to February 10, 1908, the Wrights had been scoffed at and belittled, and had been called fakers and charlatans. Scientists and government officials as well as average people in all countries could not understand how these upstart bicycle repairmen from Dayton, Ohio, could have been so bold as to claim that they had actually flown in airplanes, when the problems of powered flight had defeated some of the best technical brains in the world. Indeed, even Sir Hiram

Stevens Maxim, inventor of the machine gun, who had spent a fortune trying to develop a flying machine, had finally admitted that his research proved conclusively that "the aeroplane system is not practical for flying."

But the scoffing and the taunts were over. The Wrights had won—almost. They had their contracts, and they had only to deliver.

First came Wilbur's demonstrations at Le Mans, some 125 miles from Paris, on August 8. With the stipulated two flights, witnessed by officials of the French Government, he fulfilled the terms of the contract and all doubts were washed away. The official British observer at these flights was Major B.F.S. Baden-Powell, and he said, "That Wilbur Wright is in possession of a power which controls the fate of nations is beyond dispute."

Orville and the world's first military airplane arrived in Washington on August 20, 1908, and the following morning it was taken to Fort Myer, Virginia, in a horse-drawn Army wagon, where it was placed in a balloon shed to be assembled. Assembly was completed six days later.

The Wright Army airplane was larger and more powerful than any other machine the brothers had built, though similar in general layout to those they had flown previously. A tail-first, or canard, biplane, it weighed 1,360 pounds and had a single engine of 25 horsepower that drove two wide-bladed pusher propellers through a series of sprockets and bicycle chains. The total fuel capacity was thirteen gallons. There was a benchlike upholstered seat for the pilot and one passenger near the leading edge of the lower wing next to the engine. There were no safety belts, and the only "instrument" consisted of a short piece of string tied to a strut near the pilot, serving both as a turn-and-bank indicator and a stall-warning device.

The Wright Army airplane had parallel skids instead of wheels. The machine was designed to be catapulted by dropping a 1,500-pound counterweight in a tower behind the monorail starting track. Through the combination of catapult and

Orville Wright flying at Fort Myer, Virginia, in September 1908. The plane crashed on September 17, killing Lieutenant Thomas Selfridge, the first to die in an airplane accident.   *U.S. Air Force*

engine power, the plane was expected to attain a take-off speed of 23 miles per hour by the time it reached the end of the fifty-foot track.

Everything was finally ready by the afternoon of September 3, and Orville started his engine at 5:15 and tripped the catapult release.

A crowd of about 600 people watched breathlessly as the fragile wood-and-muslin creation started to move down the launch track, its engine roaring and its propellers spinning rapidly. After a run of about forty feet, the flying machine lifted into the air.

Orville climbed his machine to an altitude of about thirty-five feet, flying straight ahead. Then he executed a smooth bank and came back over the crowd. Near the end of the field he turned again, but this time something happened. One wing suddenly dipped sharply, and the people below gasped. A crash seemed inevitable. But Orville managed to right his wings just before the craft hit the ground with a thud and skidded across the ground in a cloud of dust. The flight had lasted only seventy seconds, and one of the skids was damaged. But Orville had done the impossible: he had proved to official Washington that the flying machine was a reality.

As a result of this one brief demonstration of mechanical flight, Brigadier General Arthur Murray, Chief of the Army's Coast Artillery, declared, "War on land and sea will find in the aeroplane a valuable means of reconnaissance and possible carnage." General Murray could not have realized how prophetic his remark was to prove to be, just as the British Major Baden-Powell before him could not have known that within a few brief years the airplane would become such a valuable tool of war.

The following day Orville was in the air again, extending the duration of his flight to five minutes. On September 7 and 8 he made other brief flights, and the next day he remained aloft for fifty-seven minutes and thirty-one seconds, which was a world's record for heavier-than-air machines. Later that same day Orville took Lieutenant Lahm for a ride—the first airplane flight by an Army officer.

"We could see Washington in the distance, and everything that went on below," Lahm said after the seven-minute flight. "I watched Wright closely as he handled the controlling apparatus. It didn't look too difficult. Flying this way was a great sensation, much different from flights in the balloons or dirigibles."

On September 12 Orville took Major George O. Squier for a ride. The major was an important passenger, for he was a member of the Army's official acceptance board. And Major Squier was deeply impressed. After they had landed, he told Orville, "If the machine is as good as it seems to be, the Army will be buying a lot of these."

Up until this time, aviation had been strictly a sport, a harmless test of man's ingenuity against the forces of nature. However, it was to be demonstrated that these natural forces could not be truly conquered.

Orville was not satisfied with the performance of his flying machine; he decided to substitute a new set of propellers, hoping that these would deliver more power. Another flight, with the new propellers installed, was made on September 17, this time with Lieutenant Thomas E. Selfridge as the passenger. On the fourth circuit of the field, at an altitude of about 180 feet, something went wrong.

The plane suddenly began to vibrate, and then there was a loud thump as one of the propellers sliced through a bracing wire. Orville cut his engine and tried desperately to maintain control. Despite his efforts, the plane crashed. Orville was injured, suffering broken ribs and a fractured thigh, and Lieutenant Selfridge was knocked unconscious. He died three hours later in Walter Reed Army Hospital. But despite this tragic accident, the interest and enthusiasm of military men in the flying machine and its future remained at a high pitch. The War Department gave the Wrights an opportunity to show them another model, and a second plane was built. It was delivered

The world's first military airplane at Fort Myer on July 27, 1909.
The flimsy machine had to be catapulted into the air, could do only
47 miles per hour with no headwind.   *U.S. Air Force*

to Fort Myer, Virginia, in July 1909, and this time all the tests went off smoothly. The final flight, with Lieutenant Benjamin D. Foulois as passenger and Orville at the controls, was a twenty-mile round-trip to Alexandria, Virginia. The machine also proved its endurance by remaining aloft for one hour, twelve minutes, and forty seconds. The official testing board reported that "in the opinion of the board the plane complied with the specifications in every respect as far as the endurance test is concerned, which required the machine to remain in the air but one hour."

The top speed of that first successful military airplane was clocked at 47 miles per hour, and its average speed in two directions over a measured course was 42.5 miles per hour. Since the Wrights had exceeded the required specifications, they were awarded a bonus of $5,000 over the contract price of $25,000.

Aeroplane No. 1, Heavier-than-air Division, United States Aerial Fleet, was formally turned over to the U.S. Signal Corps on August 2, 1909. And thus, five and a half years after the first feeble flights from the wind-swept dunes of Kitty Hawk, North Carolina, military aviation was born.

While the United States led the world in military aviation, with its one and only airplane, survival of the Aeronautical Division seemed doubtful. In the summer of 1910 Army aviation personnel consisted of two flying officers, nine enlisted men, and virtually no operating funds. In order to continue flying, in fact, there were times when the men in the Division bought their own gasoline and lubricating oil. The Chief Signal Officer repeatedly urged Congress to appropriate more funds for development, but without success. "What's all this fuss about airplanes for the Army?" one Congressman reportedly grumbled. "I thought we already had one."

Still the Signal Corps persisted in its request for more funds, and on March 3, 1911, Congress voted its very first appropriation for aeronautical development: $125,000. This made possible new equipment for training. An aviation school was also started at College Park, Maryland, where experiments were conducted in aerial photography and bomb dropping.

While Congress had loosened the purse strings, the Aeronautical Division was not pleased with the rate of progress or the machines it had in service. Indeed, the first Wright and Curtiss planes delivered could be taken aloft under only the most favorable weather conditions. They could not fly far enough or fast enough or carry a large enough load for military purposes. There were constant malfunctions, and the flying machines spent most of the time in the hangars for repairs.

The farsighted realized that the airplane could have excellent military potential, but much development would be necessary before this potential could become reality. Aviation was then only eight years old, and while ailerons had been added in place of wing-warping for lateral control, there had been very little other progress. The few stalwart pioneers had virtually no manufacturing facilities, no money for research, and little or no interest from the public. Despite these difficult conditions, some military tacticians envisioned swarms of these machines buzzing through the air and attacking enemy strongholds that could not be breached by conventional ground weapons. But while the visions were there, even the most daring could not guess about the probable appearance of these flying machines of the future.

Meanwhile, the promise of the airplane as a weapon was also being investigated in Europe. The United States had established the first military aviation division and accepted the first military airplane. This potential threat had to be matched. The gas balloon had previously been used in warfare, but it had severe limitations. The balloon could not be flown to and from specific objectives but had to drift with the wind, and the direction of the winds could not be controlled. A number of dirigibles had also been built. Count Ferdinand von Zeppelin had completed his first rigid airship, the LZ-1, and had flown it with limited success from Lake Constance, near Friedrichshafen, Germany. The indomitable Brazilian, Alberto Santos-Dumont, had also made headlines by circling the Eiffel Tower

Thought was given to arming airplanes almost from the beginning. This picture, taken in 1910, shows U.S. Army Major J.E. Fickel, who fired the first rifle in flight. The plane is a Curtiss pusher.

U.S. Air Force

in Paris in his hydrogen-inflated airship. However, these huge machines had not proved practical; they were slow and expensive, and required extensive handling facilities on the ground. The airplane, which could be flown with more positive control and was much cheaper to build and service, appeared to have the qualities that were missing in other aerial craft.

Then two events took place in 1911 which received practically no newspaper coverage but which proved to even the most stubborn skeptics that the military potential of the airplane could not be shrugged off lightly.

There was a revolution in Mexico, and American forces were stationed at the border to prevent the internal strife from spilling over and endangering United States civilians and property. The U.S. Army had one Wright biplane in Texas under the command of Lieutenant Foulois, but it was scheduled to be shipped back to the factory in Dayton, Ohio, for overhaul and repair. This gap was filled by a sportsman named Robert J. Collier, who loaned his private plane to the Army to carry on aerial reconnaissance. With Lieutenant Foulois as observer and Philip O. Parmalie, a pilot employed by the Wrights, at the controls, several observation flights were made in the vicinity of Laredo, Texas. This was the first practical application of a flying machine under operational military conditions, and while its role was strictly that of observation, intelligence-gathering has continued to be a primary function of the airplane.

Following the American lead, the Italians used several airplanes for reconnaissance duties in their 1911 war with Turkey. On November 1, a Lieutenant Gavotti electrified the military men of the world when he flew the world's first bombing mission in a monoplane designed and built by an Austrian named Igo Etrich. Eric Stuart Bruce described this raid in his book *Aircraft in War*, which was published in England in 1914:

Lieutenant Gavotti was at the time 700 feet above the oasis of Ain Zara, when he discovered beneath [him] two masses of Arabs, numbering each about 1,500 men. He took out the bomb from a bag at his side with one hand, while with the other he manoeuvred the machine, and as he passed over a group of Arabs he dropped the bomb. He could follow its course for a moment or two while he was passing over the bright green verdure of the oasis, but it was speedily lost to sight, while the noise of the motor prevented his hearing the explosion below. He saw, however, a cloud of smoke and the Arabs flying in all directions.

This was the first instance on record of bomb throwing from aircraft. Gavotti was himself of the opinion that in bomb throwing the operation should be carried out with the aid of two aeroplanes: the one in advance should throw the bomb, the one following observe the result.

Four days later the Italians dropped bombs on Arab positions again, and on November 5 they issued an historic military communiqué—the first to mention the airplane in combat:

Yesterday Capts. Moizo, Piazza, and DeRada carried out an airplane reconnaissance, DeRada successfully trying the new Farman military biplane. Moizo, after locating the position of the enemy's battery, flew over Ain Zara, and dropped two bombs into the Arab encampment. He found that the enemy were much diminished in numbers since he saw them last time. Piazza dropped two bombs on the enemy with effect.

The Italians also discovered that airplanes were not immune to attack, and that gunfire from the ground had to be taken into consideration. One pilot found, upon landing, that the fuselage of his machine had been hit by six bullets. Another pilot, Captain Montu, was severely wounded by groundfire when he was at an altitude of about 1,800 feet. This was probably the first time any airman was struck by an enemy bullet. The date was February 1, 1912.

On June 7, 1912, the new air-cooled machine gun invented by Lieutenant Colonel Isaac Newton Lewis of the U.S. Coast Artillery was given aerial trials at College Park, Maryland. The plane used in the tests was a Wright Model B, and Lieutenant Roy T. Kirtland was the pilot, while Captain Charles Chandler, seated next to him, fired the gun at a white bedsheet spread out

Captain Charles Chandler fired the first machine gun from an airplane on June 7, 1912. The pilot was Lieutenant Roy Kirtland, and the tests were made at College Park, Maryland.   *U.S. Air Force*

on the grass.

The flying machine had been proved in combat and a practical method had been found to arm it. Until the invention of the Lewis gun, all machine guns had been bulky, water-cooled devices. Colonel Lewis had concluded that the constant flow of air across the barrel would provide sufficient cooling. His gun weighed twenty-six and a half pounds and had a rate of fire of 560 rounds per minute and a magazine with a capacity of forty-seven cartridges. This same basic gun was used on many Allied airplanes throughout World War I and for a number of subsequent years. It was gradually improved during the war. In July 1916 the original magazine was replaced by a double drum containing ninety-seven rounds, and by 1918 it had been modified to achieve a rate of fire of some 700 to 750 rounds per minute, while its weight was reduced to eighteen and a half pounds.

College Park continued to be the hub of aviation activity in the United States. By November 1, 1912, the size of the Aeronautical Division of the Signal Corps had increased to twelve flying officers and thirty-nine enlisted men, with twelve assorted airplanes, no two of which were identical. An old Cadillac, which had been used by General Allen, was loaned to the Division to carry cans of gasoline and to ferry the mechanics and pilots back and forth. Until 1913, this was the air arm's sole means of transport.

In February 1913, College Park was abandoned in favor of Texas City, Texas, where flying weather was more favorable on a year-round basis. The following month Congress provided 35 percent extra pay for flying personnel and set officer strength at thirty. Several bills were also introduced to elevate the Division to a branch basis, to make it equal, rather than subordinate, to the Signal Corps. All of these bills were defeated. But before the year was out, this embryonic air force had grown to fifteen planes, twenty-three officers, and ninety-one enlisted men.

The First Aero Squadron—the first United States tactical

aviation unit—was organized at San Diego, California, in December 1913. It consisted of sixteen officers, seventy-seven enlisted men, and six airplanes.

Progress had been made, but at a price. From 1909 to the end of 1913, the Signal Corps had purchased a total of twenty-four airplanes. Of these, ten had been destroyed in accidents, resulting in twelve fatalities. The records indicated that the toll had been one death for each 100 hours of flying. Six of these deaths had been in antiquated Wright Model C biplanes, which had no protective devices.

Muddled thinking in official Washington had done much to delay progress. The men behind the desks still refused to give the Wrights credit for the invention of the airplane, casting their vote instead for Professor Samuel Pierpont Langley of the Smithsonian Institution. This same sort of thinking had previously forced Hiram Maxim to emigrate to England in order to sell his celebrated machine gun. Colonel Lewis was also unsuccessful in generating interest in his aerial machine gun in his own country, and he took it to Europe, where he set up the Armes Automatiques Lewis in Belgium. Another American who had to go abroad to sell his weapon was Benjamin Hotchkiss.

Progress, mainly because of officialdom, was painfully slow in the United States. But across the Atlantic Ocean, aviation development was proceeding at a more rapid pace. The first rumblings of World War I were already sounding unmistakably in the distance. No one knew what place the airplane would have in the conflict, but the ancient enemies were getting ready, studying new ways to kill and destroy, preparing for the holocaust which at that point was nothing more ominous than harsh words and bitter accusations between opposing rulers over economic markets, boundary lines, and other such matters.

Wings Grow Stronger

Chapter Two

UNLIKE THE AMERICANS, the French accepted aviation almost from the moment that Albert Santos-Dumont, a Brazilian who had emigrated to Paris, made the first successful flights in Europe during the summer and fall of 1906. And while even the first Wright military airplane delivered to the Aeronautical Division of the Signal Corps in 1909 did not have wheels and had to be launched through the use of a catapult device, Santos-Dumont rose into the air in his No. 14*bis* after running along the ground on wheels.

The Brazilian's first flights were little more than short hops similar to those of the Wrights at Kitty Hawk. But after having Gabriel and Charles Voisin build him a second machine, which was similar in general layout to the first, he switched to a tiny monoplane weighing only 260 pounds. This plane, which Santos-Dumont called the *Demoiselle*, had a wing span of only 18 feet and a length of 17 feet. The engine was a 28-horsepower air-cooled Darracq with two cylinders. The *Demoiselle* was the world's first ultralight airplane, and it looked more like a toy than an actual flying machine. There was no fuselage as such, but merely a triangular bamboo frame. The pilot sat in the framework, cramped under the wing, with his feet drawn up on the axle to which the wheels were attached.

Another remarkable French airplane to appear in 1908 was the Antoinette, which was designed by Léon Levasseur. A sleek, graceful monoplane, it mounted a 50-horsepower Antoinette engine, which was the most reliable power plant built in the country up to that time. With Hubért Latham at the controls the Antoinette set several records; among others, it became the first airplane to reach an altitude of 500 feet. Latham twice attempted to fly across the English Channel in the Antoinette, but he fell short on both occasions—on June 29, 1909, by only a mile. Louis Blériot finally made the crossing successfully the following month in a plane of his own design but powered by the Antoinette engine. Santos-Dumont's first machines also used this engine.

Another Frenchman working independently of government funds was Robert Esnault-Pelterie, whose designs were amazingly different from those of the other pioneers. Equally amazing is the fact that Esnault-Pelterie's name has been all but lost in the history of aviation, since he was without doubt one of the most influential of all the early designers. One of his contributions was the discovery that the drag of exposed wires, struts, and other such braces lowered performance, and that their presence in the slipstream resulted in a substantial loss of usable engine power. An illustration of how far ahead of his time Esnault-Pelterie actually was is that even twenty years later every major military power was still using biplane fighters and bombers replete with struts, wires, and other bracing out in the slipstream and creating drag!

Working with his own funds, the brilliant French designer as far back as 1909 built a beautiful monoplane with a welded steel-tubing fuselage and internally braced wooden wings, both with fabric covering. Virtually no protuberances jutted into the slipstream from his R.E.P., which used a 30-horse-power engine. A later version of this machine, with the 60-horsepower Le Rhone rotary engine, had a maximum speed of 75 miles per hour.

There were numerous other notable French developments

Louis Blériot altered the original monoplane which he flew across the English Channel to produce the XI *Militaire*. This was the first military airplane in France. *National Archives*

The Farman S.7 Longhorn was a mass of struts and wires and could do only 59 miles per hour. However, it was to see considerable service in the early days of the war. *"Flight"*

during this prewar period. Among these were the planes built by Gabriel and Charles Voisin. The firm had actually been started by Gabriel Voisin, and by 1906 he had established himself as a builder of "custom aircraft," specializing in fabricating planes to the specifications of other pioneers—among whom were Alberto Santos-Dumont and Louis Blériot. After Charles joined his brother Gabriel, they made the first wind tunnel in Europe to test their designs. During this time the first joystick control appeared in the cockpit of a Voisin-built plane, though the patent for the device was taken out by Blériot as an improvement of a control system worked out previously by Alphonse Pénaud, another Frenchman.

The Voisin brothers also built an airplane of their design for Henri Farman, who later opened his own factory and produced machines that were similar in general layout to his first Voisin. Maurice Farman also gained considerable recognition as a designer, though his planes were similar to those his brother designed. While the Farman brothers designed their aircraft independently, all were produced at the same factory at Billancourt, France. One of Maurice Farman's first successful designs was the S.7, which was followed by the S.11; these were better known as the Longhorn and the Shorthorn. The names came about when a French general, after seeing the planes for the first time, referred to them as mechanical cows. The S.7, with its long outriggers and elevator located in front, became the Longhorn; while the S.11, which had no such arrangement, was called the Shorthorn.

Despite their ugliness, the Farman planes not only set the style for British aeronautical engineering, but also helped to further aviation progress. In 1909, the world's endurance record was set at four hours and seventeen minutes in a Henri Farman, covering a distance of 145 miles. In 1913, a Maurice Farman flew nonstop for thirteen hours and twenty-two minutes, while one of his brother's designs went 634 miles.

While the French were experimenting with various shapes and types of airplanes, they were training pilots faster than any other country. At the beginning of 1911 the number of certified pilots in each of the principal countries were:

France	353	Italy	32
England	57	Belgium	27
Germany	46	United States	26

This progress was not made without some initial opposition from the government, for while the French had been the first to buy rights to the Wright brothers' patents, they had been reluctant to order military aircraft into production. The French General Staff at that time put more faith in the dirigible than it did in the airplane, and the few officers who were interested in flying machines were considered not quite right in the head.

The most outspoken of these officers was Captain Ferdinand Ferber. Ferber had been associated with the Wrights after their first experiments, and he was such an avid advocate of aviation in his own country, to the obvious displeasure of his superiors, that in order to continue flying he had to do so under an assumed name.

However, a change was coming. The success of the international Flying Week at Reims in August 1909 brought about a great spurt in aeronautical interest. Here, for the first time, the military became convinced that the flying machine would play an important role in the war which seemed to be just ahead. Because of this, General Brun, the Minister of War, decided to purchase a few airplanes for the army.

During the following year the French started extensive tests with airplanes. They tried them as spotters for artillery, for reconnaissance during maneuvers to uncover troop movements, and for experiments in aerial photography.

The results of these tests were not as good as had been expected. The planes could fly only under ideal weather conditions, required more care than had been anticipated, and suffered too many engine failures and consequent forced landings. As a result, the War Department decided to hold a military-aircraft competition. Among other things, they insisted that to be eligible, planes entered would be required to fly at least 186 miles nonstop with a military payload of 660 pounds, and that they would have to maintain an average speed of at least 37 miles per hour. One hundred and ten builders announced their intention to submit entries following publication of the specifications. When the deadline arrived, however, only thirty-two were actually presented for inspection. Of these, only nine passed the preliminary tests required for the final competition on November 1, 1911.

The rapid growth of aviation in France, after a bad start, is illustrated by the number of airplanes submitted for this one military competition, which had been called on such short notice that a number of designs were not ready in time for the specified entry date. Two years later the French were able to export 285 airplanes plus spare parts. By comparison, production of aircraft in the United States for the entire year of 1914 amounted to only forty-nine—and this was more than the number completed in any year prior to that time.

French advances were so impressive that it is difficult to chronicle each of these. However, here are some of the highlights:

In 1910 Edouard and Charles Nieuport built a monoplane with a steel-tubing fuselage and fabric covering. C.T. Weyman, an American, flew this ship to win the Gordon Bennett air race at a speed of 78 miles per hour. Two years later, flying a Morane-Saulnier monoplane, Roland Garros set a new altitude record of 18,400 feet. The altitude record in the United States at this time was 11,642 feet. That same year the Déperdussin monoplanes with plywood fuselages were the fastest and most eye-appealing in the world. These beautiful little machines were the result of design work by M.L. Béchereau and a young Dutchman named Fritz Koolhoven. That year in Chicago, Illinois, in the Gordon Bennett race, the Déperdussins displayed their superiority by capturing first and second places, with Jules Védrines winning at a speed of 105 miles per hour

The Nieuport monoplane was the world's fastest airplane in 1910, with a maximum speed of about 90 miles per hour. The plane set a new standard of design.   *French Official*

for the 125 miles. This was definitely no airplane for a fledgling to fly, for its landing speed was 90 miles per hour, very fast compared to its top speed of about 115. The following year an improved Déperdussin returned to the Bennett race, this time trouncing all opposition as it recorded a speed of 124.8 miles per hour.

The French were also experimenting with the airplane as an offensive weapon. In 1912 they sent pilots and planes to Algeria to test them under desert-flying conditions. That same year other planes were sent to Morocco, and in January 1913 these were used for reconnaissance and ground attack against the Moroccan rebels.

At the same time, the French had developed the most efficient and reliable aircraft engines known anywhere in the world. In addition to the Antoinette, the most notable of these was the Gnome, designed and built by Laurent and Louis Seguin. The Gnome was entirely different from any aircraft engine produced up to that time. Called a rotary, the entire engine revolved at the same speed as the propeller. This resulted in a torque effect, giving the plane in which it was installed a tendency to turn because of the rotation of the engine. Despite this drawback, the Gnome was able to deliver more horsepower for its weight than any other engine, primarily because there was no heavy crankshaft. There were no finer engines at the time than the Gnome, nor any that were more dependable. By 1911, the Gnome was delivering 100 horsepower, and in the latter part of 1913 the 140-horsepower version was introduced.

Meanwhile, the Armand Déperdussin company produced a two-seat monoplane for military use, basing its general design on their racers. This plane was the finest machine in the air and presented a challenge to all other designers. The Déperdussin firm, the full name of which was Société pour les Appareils Déperdussin, went bankrupt in 1913. Shortly thereafter the organization was taken over by Louis Blériot, and he renamed it the Société pour Aviation et ses Dérivés, thus preserving the original initials. Béchereau and Koolhoven were retained as the designing team. The abbreviation of the firm name was usually lettered on the rudders of the planes it produced: S.P.A.D. This became the renowned Spad, which so many Allied pilots flew during World War I.

Another French design that must be mentioned is that of Léon and Robert Morane, who were later joined by Raymond Saulnier, a true engineering genius. This combination of talents resulted in some of the finest airplanes available to the French military. Among these were the Morane-Saulnier Model L and Model N. The Model L, which appeared in 1913, can claim to be the world's first true fighter plane. A parasol design —that is, the monoplane wing was entirely above and removed from the fuselage, attached only by struts—it mounted the 80-horsepower Gnome rotary engine and clocked out at 72 miles per hour.

The Model N came closer to the true configuration of a fighter plane. It was remarkably well streamlined with the monoplane wing placed in the midfuselage position. With the 110-horsepower Le Rhone rotary (which was similar to the Gnome), it had a maximum speed of 102 miles per hour at 6,500 feet. This plane was also known as the Bullet, and in the war days just ahead, with Roland Garros in the cockpit, it was to become famous in aerial combat.

Aviation in these days was still in its infancy in the United States, Britain, and Germany. But in France the infant had been given muscle and was rapidly growing to a maturity which few would have thought possible in such a short period of time. And now, very soon, those muscles were to be put to the test.

No airplane in the world could compare favorably with the Déperdussin of 1912. It was the first flying machine to exceed 100 miles
per hour in level flight.   *National Archives*

Teething Troubles in England

Chapter Three

Across the English Channel in Great Britain, government leaders were also concerned about the intentions of Kaiser Wilhelm II and had started to bolster their fighting forces. The British, like the Americans, had at first lagged in aeronautical development, and most military leaders refused to concede that the airplane could become useful in the foreseeable future. In fact, Captain Bertram Dickson, the first British officer to fly, had done so in a Henri Farman biplane he bought in France with his own money.

Then, on February 28, 1911, primarily because of the aeronautical activity in France, a British army order was issued which called for organizing an Air Battalion of the Royal Engineers "to which will be entrusted the duty of creating a body of expert airmen." The order further stated that the new unit would be responsible for "the training and instruction of men in handling kites, balloons, aeroplanes, and other forms of aircraft." The airplane company of the Battalion was placed under the command of Captain J.D.B. Fulton, and his equipment

Perhaps the most amazing feature of the Bristol Boxkite was that it managed to fly at all. With a 50 horsepower engine, it had a maximum speed of only 37 miles per hour.   *U.S. Air Force*

consisted of a total of five Bristol Boxkites and Henri Farmans, one of which was owned by the pilot himself.

The most amazing feature of the Bristol was that it managed to stagger into the air at all. It had been well named: it bristled with wires and struts every place imaginable. Maximum speed was 37 miles per hour with an air-cooled rotary engine rated at 50 horsepower. In those early days the firm that manufactured these machines was officially known as the British and Colonial Aeroplane Company of Filton near Bristol. In comparison with the Boxkite, the Henri Farman was a sturdy and reliable machine. With an 80-horsepower Gnome rotary engine, it carried a crew of two at a maximum speed of 65 miles per hour.

With this motley equipment, the Air Battalion was ordered to participate in the army maneuvers of 1911. Four of the five machines started on a "cross-country" flight of about fifty-five miles, the other plane having crashed the previous day. Of the four, two were quickly eliminated by accidents, one of which is an aviation classic.

Lieutenant Reynolds, the pilot of the Boxkite, encountered unexpected rough weather and quickly concluded that he would be better off on the ground. He went into a glide to land in a farmyard, when suddenly the turbulent wind flipped his machine upside down and also bounced Reynolds from his seat, depositing him on the *underside* of what was normally the upper wing. Reynolds held on grimly while his Boxkite did a slow roll, then a tail slide, and, finally, a falling leaf to the ground, still in the inverted position. Luck was with Lieutenant Reynolds, and he managed to jump the last ten feet, suffering nothing more than minor bruises and scrapes—plus injured pride—before his Bristol crashed.

But there was irony yet to come. When the two remaining airplanes arrived at their destination, the pilots discovered to their chagrin that the maneuvers had been canceled.

After this exercise, the Air Battalion was reduced to two airplanes. However, the pioneers persisted, and toward the end of

1911 Captain Dickson wrote an official memorandum which read:

> In the case of a European war between two countries, both sides would be equipped with large corps of aeroplanes, each trying to obtain information of the other, and to hide its own movements. The efforts which each would exert in order to hinder or prevent the enemy from obtaining information would lead to the inevitable result of a war in the air, for the supremacy of the air, by armed aeroplanes against each other. This fight for the supremacy of the air in future wars will be of the first and greatest importance.

No one can tell what influence this memorandum had, if any, on the members of the Committee of Imperial Defence, but the British realized that a flying force would have to be developed for what seemed to be an inevitable war. A Royal Warrant dated April 13, 1912, was a step in the right direction, changing the name of the Air Battalion to Royal Flying Corps. That same year a competition for military airplanes was also held.

During these trials the *Cody Cathedral* built by Samuel Franklin Cody, a Texan by birth who had become a British citizen, easily took top honors. However, his creation, which was huge, ungainly, and obviously unsuited for military operations, was bypassed in favor of the B.E.2 built by the Royal Aircraft Factory at Farnborough.

The B.E.2 had been designed by Geoffrey de Havilland, a brilliant young man who was later to become famous for his military and commercial aircraft. But while the B.E.2 was a good machine for its day and did important reconnaissance work during the early months of the war, it was a failure under combat conditions and a favorite target of German fighter pilots. The plane had tandem cockpits, with the pilot in the rear and the observer in the front, where he was so completely surrounded by wings, wires, struts, and engine that he could look downward only over the leading edge of the lower wing, or by twisting around in his seat and peering back over the trailing edge of the wing.

The first competition for military planes in England was won by the cumbersome *Cody Cathedral*. Since the machine was unsuited for military operations, it was not ordered.   *U.S. Air Force*

In its original configuration, the B.E.2 mounted a 70-horse-power Renault engine. Its maximum speed under ideal conditions was 72 miles per hour, and it required an hour and twenty minutes to climb to an altitude of 9,500 feet.

When the B.E.2 was first produced the system of designation for aircraft had just been initiated. At the time many people believed that B.E. meant British Experimental, but this was not so. The designation actually meant Blériot Experimental—not because Louis Blériot had had anything to do with the design, but in deference to his system of placing the engine and propeller in front in the tractor position rather than in the rear in the pusher position. It was not until later that B.E. came to mean British Experimental and F.E. (originally Farman Experimental, for pushers) became Fighter Experimental.

Britain had finally started to build an air force, but one type of airplane was obviously not enough. The French had produced the Morane-Saulnier L and several other specialized types, and the British knew they had to keep pace. Again with de Havilland as designer, the Royal Aircraft Factory rolled out a trim little single-seat biplane that was far ahead of its time. This was the B.S.1 (Blériot Scout), which was to become the forerunner of the famous S.E. series of later years.

The B.S.1 was built to obtain experimental data for a high-speed scouting airplane. Provision was originally made to install the 140-horsepower twin-row Gnome rotary engine, but the 100-horsepower ten-cylinder version was actually used. With a fuel supply sufficient for three hours, it had a speed of 92 miles per hour and an initial rate of climb of 900 feet per minute. The plane crashed in March 1913, but damage was not extensive and it was rebuilt as the S.E.2 Bullet, the initials now meaning Scouting Experimental. The S.E.2 had a smaller engine—the 80-horsepower Gnome—plus other modifications, including a vertical fin in front of the rudder. The reduced power lowered the maximum speed to 85 miles per hour and the rate of climb to 780 feet per minute. However, the modifications turned it into a better, more reliable airplane.

Britain's first true military airplane was the B.E.2, which was designed by Geoffrey de Havilland. In its original form, it could do only 72 miles per hour in calm air.   *"Flight"*

The most successful British airplane prior to the war was the Sopwith Tabloid. The machine had its official trials in November 1913 and was immediately ordered. *Imperial War Museum*

The B.S.1 was actually the first fighter-type airplane produced in England, but this distinction is usually erroneously
given to the Tabloid designed by T.O.M. Sopwith, which also
appeared in 1913. The biplane Tabloid mounted the 80-horse-
power Gnome rotary engine and had a maximum speed of 92
miles per hour and a climbing rate of 1,200 feet per minute.

The Tabloid had its first official trials at Farnborough on
November 29, 1913, and it created a sensation. The following
month it was demonstrated in a closed-course race in competition with several monoplanes, and it easily won all the speed
and performance events. This spirited little single-seater was
to earn fame in the coming war not as a fighter, but as a bomber.

During this period the British made a number of attempts
to arm their airplanes, with varying results. The first recorded
attempt seems to have been by Major Brooke-Popham of the
Air Battalion, who in 1911 fitted a machine gun to a Blériot
monoplane but was quickly ordered to remove it. This order
was probably issued because of a General Staff memorandum
which stated, in part, that there was "no great likelihood of
aerial scouts coming into conflict." At that time, the British
Army thought of using airplanes only for reconnaissance.

In 1913, however, the War Office decided that some experiments would have to be made. The Royal Aircraft Factory
fitted Hotchkiss machine guns to two or three Henri Farman
biplanes, and during the spring of that year tests were conducted. These tests proved, contrary to theories that had been
advanced by some skeptics, that the recoil of a machine gun
fired from an airplane in flight had no appreciable effect on its
stability. It was also found that the Hotchkiss gun was unsuit-
able, and that guns used on aircraft would have to be fully
automatic to be really effective.

Several other tests were conducted, the most notable of
which took place on November 27, 1913. The airplane in this
case was a Grahame-White with a 50-horsepower engine. Mar-
cus Manton was the pilot, and the gunner was Lieutenant

Stellingwerf of the Belgian Army, who was actually acting as salesman for the Lewis gun.

During these trials, the Grahame-White made two passes over a ground target consisting of a cotton sheet about twenty-five feet square. On the first pass, from an average distance of about 900 feet, Stellingwerf managed to hit the sheet eleven times with the twenty-five bullets fired. During the second pass, at the same average distance, he scored fifteen times out of forty-seven rounds.

Following these tests, Lieutenant Clark-Hall, the Armament Officer, stated that in his opinion the chief function of machine guns mounted on airplanes would not be for attack against targets on the ground, but for shooting at other aircraft.

About the same time as these latter tests were being made, another British plane was produced which was to become famous. This was the Vickers F.B. (Fighting Biplane) Gun Bus. As early as 1912 the Vickers firm realized that it would be necessary for aircraft to carry guns into battle. The F.B.2 was the result. This machine was the world's first to be designed specifically for aerial fighting, with the gunner sitting forward of the pilot in the nacelle, which held the engine as well as the crew. In its original version, the F.B.2 mounted a .303-caliber Maxim machine gun with a belt feed. However, this was not successful, and the lighter Lewis gun was substituted.

A pusher biplane, the Gun Bus was much more of an airplane than its appearance seemed to indicate. While the wings and nacelle were covered with fabric, the tail surfaces were suspended on outrigging. In many ways the Gun Bus appeared to be little more than a variation of the Farman designs. When it was taken into the air, however, it proved to be something else again.

Many people smiled knowingly when they first saw the machine, with the conviction that it would most likely vibrate to bits as soon as the machine gun was fired. In actual fact, the Gun Bus not only remained intact from the recoil of its gun but was to become the backbone of the Royal Flying Corps in 1915.

In its F.B.5 version, the Gun Bus mounted the 100-horse-power Gnome engine; it climbed to 5,000 feet in sixteen minutes, where it had a maximum speed of 70 miles per hour. It was hardly the fastest airplane in the skies, but as later events were to prove—even in the final stages of the air war—speed was not as important as flying and handling characteristics.

That the Gun Bus did not go into immediate production was a fact which disturbed British flyers greatly during the initial phases of the war. As things were, the War Office was in favor of using airplanes built by the government, and the Royal Aircraft Factory was instructed to produce a smiliar design. This model was known as the F.E.2b, the first models of which were unsatisfactory because of their troublesome Beardmore engines.

In April 1909 the British War Office had announced that it "had decided to cease making any experiments with aeroplanes as the cost had proved too great." The total amount spent on military airplanes up to that time had been approximately $7,500. But now, with war right around the corner, they were working under pressure and trying to do things in a week that should have been done in a year. And many mistakes were being made. One mistake was to build the B.E.2 at all, for shortly it was to become a flying coffin for many brave pilots and the plane that gave birth to the phrase "Fokker Fodder." Other mistakes were that they did not rush the S.E.2, Tabloid, or F.B.5 into production. But despite such early mistakes British airplanes and the men of the Royal Flying Corps eventually proved to be the equal of any air force in the world.

Growing Pains
in Germany

Chapter Four

WHILE PROGRESS WAS BEING MADE at a rapid rate in France, slowly in England, and at a snail's pace in the United States, development of the airplane as a weapon of war was practically nonexistent in Germany. As early as 1910 the German Government had allocated some $2,000,000 for development of military aviation, whereas the French had spent $245,000 and the British only approximately $25,000. But while the Germans were spending more money, most of it was used to build the huge rigid airships designed by Graf Ferdinand von Zeppelin. Fixed-wing airplanes in Germany at that time were little better than copies of Wright, Farman, Blériot, and other designs. Indeed, one of the first Germans to fly, Hans Grade, combined in his frail machine the best features of the Santos-Dumont, Blériot, and Antoinette machines. This in the country where the great pioneer, Otto Lilienthal, had come so close to mastering powered flight and had sparked the Wrights on to final success!

The first attempt in Germany to build a military airplane was entrusted to a government architect named W.G. Hoffman. He obviously knew nothing about aerodynamics and did little more than copy the Wright biplane, but for some reason he failed to add a rudder. The machine crashed during its trial flight.

The German Air Force started to fly on October 1, 1910—but its single airplane, a Farman pusher, was borrowed from Dr. Fritz Huth. When this machine crashed early the following year, there could be no further flying.

The first German airplane to gain distinction as a military machine was the Taube (Dove) designed by Igo Etrich. A native Austrian, Etrich tried to sell his airplane to his own government, but it was turned down. A short time later the Taube design was purchased by Edmund Rumpler, who had started an aircraft factory near Berlin.

A monoplane, the Taube quickly attracted the military, as Rumpler had anticipated. Mounting a variety of engines, from the 75-horsepower Schwabe to the 100-horsepower Mercedes or Argus, the Taube had a maximum speed of from 50 to 55 miles per hour.

The Taube continued for several months as not only the best but also the only German military airplane. It was produced by several different factories. One version from D.F.W. (Deutsche Flugzeug-Werke) had a steel-tubing fuselage and a slightly larger wing span, yet was able to do 72 miles per hour with the 100-horsepower Mercedes. However, the Rumpler model surpassed all others in general performance, and one of these was flown to a new altitude record of nearly 20,000 feet.

Then, late in 1911, the German War Ministry—primarily because of the rapid advances in France—finally realized that perhaps it would be wise to investigate the flying machine in more depth. General Graf Helmuth von Moltke insisted, "We must proceed to intensify our efforts if we wish to overtake the obvious material inferiority under which we suffer in this department of our defenses in comparison with our Western neighbor. It will only be by extraordinary efforts on our part

One of the original Taubes designed by Igo Etrich. Until the advent
of the Taube in 1910, the German Air Force was equipped with
Wright biplanes and copies of French types.   *U.S. Air Force*

The first military planes built by the Albatros Flugzeug-werke were copies of French Farmans. This 1911 design was also powered by a French Renault engine of 60 horsepower. *U.S. Air Force*

that we can get the lead again, a lead which is of vital importance to our operations."

Partly as a result of Moltke's insistence, the War Ministry
issued a request for airplanes. The specifications required that
to be eligible for the competition, aircraft submitted could have
wing spans of no more than 50 feet, fuselage lengths of a maximum of 40 feet, and heights of no more than 13 feet. Further
requirements were that the planes have a minimum flying range
of four hours, a maximum of 100 horsepower, a speed of at
least 56 miles per hour, and the capability of carrying bombs
and photographic equipment.

Such requirements were fairly normal, but there were other
requirements which were different from bids that had been
issued to manufacturers in other countries. The War Ministry
insisted that the aircraft submitted must be not only entirely of
German manufacture, with no components coming from other
countries, but that they "have comfortable seats for the pilot
and passenger" so that unnecessary fatigue would not result
during a long flight.

By this time the German Air Force consisted of four Rumpler
Taubes and an assortment of other types, including a Farman-
inspired biplane produced by the Albatros-Werke. But while
there were virtually no airplanes, a request to the German
Army for volunteers for the Air Force was answered by more
than 900 officers. This was a far greater number than could be
accepted, for as Colonel Morgenstern-Doering said, "We must
have a few officers left for the infantry!"

Perhaps the most progressive German aircraft designer in
this early period was a young engineer named Ernst Heinkel,
who had flown—and crashed—his first flying machine on July
19, 1911. As Heinkel lay in the hospital recovering from various
broken bones, he decided to devote the rest of his life to aviation.

After studying construction techniques and aerodynamics,
Heinkel decided that the monoplane offered the best promise
for performance. However, the monoplanes then being built

The Albatros B-2 of 1913 was designed by Ernst Heinkel. The pilot sat in the rear cockpit, with the observer up front. The B-2 was Germany's best observation plane early in the war.

were crashing regularly, and the War Ministry had said it was interested only in biplanes, which were assumed to be safer.

Heinkel went to work for the L.V.G. firm (Luftverkehrs Gesellschaft), and his first design, a biplane, was entered in the 1912 military competition. A two-seater, it was powered by the six-cylinder Mercedes engine and had a maximum speed of 56 miles per hour. While this speed barely met the requirements, the plane was accepted for service because of its excellent flying characteristics.

After designing his first L.V.G., Heinkel moved on to the Albatros-Werke. It seems, from his autobiography, *He. 1000,* that he made his move for two reasons: because of the urging of his old friend Hellmuth Hirth, who was the most famous pilot in Germany, and because the partner in the firm, Otto Wiener, gave his permission for Heinkel to build monoplanes.

Heinkel's first machine for Albatros was the B-1, a beautiful midwing monoplane with an oval wooden fuselage and a semi-cantilever wing. It was fitted with a 75-horsepower Mercedes engine. This machine set several records for speed and endurance, and it was the first German plane to execute a loop without falling apart. Despite this performance, the B-1 was not ordered by the German army. However, an amphibian version with twin floats and wheels was later put into limited production for the navy.

The first Heinkel-designed machine to be accepted by the army was the Albatros B-2 biplane, which won the military competition in 1913. This design was unique in that it could be fitted with wings of different span for such purposes as high-altitude flight and general reconnaissance. With the shorter wings, it had a maximum speed of 69 miles per hour.

Meanwhile, a Dutchman named Anthony Fokker became disgruntled when his own country refused to buy airplanes from him. He tried England next, and again he was turned down. A few years later, when Fokker monoplanes held virtual control over the war in the air, an investigation was held in

England to determine why the Dutchman's design had not been bought. The answer, very simply, was that "Fokker had nothing worth having at the time."

Fokker was only about twenty years old when he moved to Germany. He had been experimenting with aviation for about two years and had built only one plane, which he called the *Spider*.

The German military had turned down other builders who submitted monoplanes, but they had a change of heart when Fokker introduced his E-1 *eindecker*. His machine was supposedly a copy of the French Morane-Saulnier Model N, but whether this was true, the *eindecker* was to figure importantly in the history of combat aviation. With an air-cooled rotary Oberursel engine of 80 horsepower, it had a top speed of 82 miles per hour and a service ceiling of 16,000 feet. The same general design was carried through the E-2, E-3, and E-4, with the wing span decreasing progressively and the speed increasing to 100 miles per hour.

During this period the Germans introduced a designation system for aircraft that was far superior to those used in other countries. Over the war years the system was gradually modified and enlarged, as various types of airplanes were produced for more specialized duties. The planes were designated as follows:

A—unarmed monoplane, mostly of the Taube class;
B—at first a biplane trainer or reconnaissance craft;
C—armed observation plane or day bomber;
D—single-seat biplane fighter;
Dr—single-seat triplane fighter;
E—single-seat monoplane fighter;
J—armored plane for ground attack;
N—night bomber;
R—large multiengined bomber;
S—ground strafer (in addition to the J);
V or W—seaplane.

There were a few other miscellaneous designations, but these craft were generally built in smaller numbers, and few became prominent.

As the air war became intense and aircraft designing developed into something approaching a science, the Germans carried their designation system to a high degree of perfection, which was not reached in other countries for many years. An example was a Fokker D-7 surrendered to the Allies under the terms of the Armistice. This machine had the following designation lettered on its fuselage: *Fok D-VII (Alb) 6786/18*. This meant that the plane was a biplane single-seat fighter designed by Fokker, the seventh type of aircraft in this class to be accepted for production by the Fokker company, that it had been built under license by Albatros, and that it was the 6,786th airplane built and delivered in 1918. Most Allied aircraft also carried designations and serial numbers, but these were not nearly as revealing.

While France concentrated most of its aircraft engine development in the prewar period on the rotary, Germany preferred the water-cooled engines with stationary cylinders. These were generally heavier per horsepower delivered and also required a considerable amount of water for cooling purposes; but they did not create the gyroscopic effect of the rotaries, and thus the airplanes in which they were installed were better flying platforms without tricky turning tendencies. At that time the Mercedes-Daimler racing cars were the fastest in the world, with the Benz designs not far behind. With these excellent power plants at their immediate disposal, it was only logical that the Germans made the decision they did. The sole exception was the Oberursel rotary, which was then used in the Fokker E-1. Many writers have claimed that the Oberursel was a copy of the French Le Rhone. This is untrue. The Oberursel was a factory-approved *duplicate* of the Gnome. The French brothers Seguin, designers of the Gnome, had set up manufacturing facilities in Britain and Germany as well as in their native land. Oberursel was merely the German name of the parent company, just as later, in Britain, the Clerget was an adaptation of the original Gnome.

The same applies to the myth that the Germans were alone in copying everything they could find of value, from the Maxim machine gun to balanced ailerons. It is often noted that in the year before the outbreak of hostilities German military airplanes included, in addition to home-produced models, several British Bristols, French Farmans, and other assorted types. But while it is true that the Germans bought and inspected airplanes built by their European neighbors—even then considered economic oppressors if not indeed enemies—and adapted advances for their own designs, the reverse is also true. At least one Albatros and several Taubes were sold to France, and the Daimler company was exporting magnetoes and other parts both to Britain and France. In those days the science of aviation was a matter of trial and error, and each bit of new information was eagerly grabbed at by designers, no matter what the source.

There was only one constant truth in Europe in those days: the day of battle was growing closer. Only a spark was needed to set off the gunpowder being produced in each of the major countries. No one could have guessed that the spark would be generated through the long-standing disputes between Austria-Hungary and Serbia. But if Archduke Francis Ferdinand, heir to the throne of Austria-Hungary, had not been assassinated by a Serbian on June 28, 1914, the great powers would have found another excuse. The war had been coming for a long time—ever since Germany defeated France in their 1870–71 war. This time, after many lesser incidents, the spark was to ignite the first flames, which quickly spread.

The gods of war could not be denied. The ancient hatreds were too great, the bitterness and rivalry too strong.

Into the Maw of Battle

Chapter Five

ON FEBRUARY 1, 1915, the Smithsonian Institution in Washington, D.C., issued a memorandum to Congress, which stated, among other things, that "when the European war broke out, France had about 1,400 airplanes, Germany 1,000, Great Britain 400, the United States 23."

This report, even coming from the respected Smithsonian, was as full of errors as were many other tables of comparative aerial strength at the time, and as have been many more since. It is a matter of historical record that when the guns started firing every country involved was in a sad condition as regards airplanes, and there was not a single plane anywhere of true military caliber. There was not one armed airplane in the sky; and the squadrons of the warring nations were composed of flying machines which most infantry generals did not want and did not know how to use. To them, war was a matter of traditional troop movements, with each side trying to outthink and outmaneuver the other. They had no use for the smelly, noisy airplane which was so undependable and required such a great amount of care and servicing. Besides, everybody knew the fighting would be over by Christmas.

At the outbreak of hostilities, the Germans had a total of forty-nine sections of six airplanes each, including eighteen home stations. This would seem to indicate a strength of 294 airplanes. However, this is higher than the actual number available. Germany was able to put only thirty-three field detachments plus eight fortress detachments into operation, with an authorized strength of 230 aircraft. Since few of these were up to full strength, the number of machines available was 218. Another forty-eight planes, which had been damaged in accidents but could be repaired, were in workshops. Of the 218 flying airplanes, only 180 could be put into the field.

French aerial strength was also greatly inflated. In August 1914 the French Air Force was composed of twenty-one *escadrilles* of two-seaters, six to the *escadrille*, plus four cavalry *escadrilles* of single-seaters, each with four planes. Assuming full strength for each of these units, the French would have had 142 aircraft. The true strength was 136, and many of these were antiquated.

The British Royal Flying Corps was numerically stronger than the French, with 179 aircraft. There were also thirty-nine landplanes and fifty-two seaplanes operational with the Royal Naval Air Service. But this combined total of 270 is misleading, since only about one-fourth of them were capable of making the short flight across the English Channel to France.

With the total Belgian strength of twenty-four added to the French and British totals, the Western Allies had approximately 210 airplanes against the Germans' 180.

It is impossible to state accurately which side first started using the airplane in connection with ground operations. One story is that the first aerial contact between the Germans and French was on August 12, when a Taube and a Morane-Saulnier passed each other at 5,000 feet, "the two pilots waving cheerfully to each other as each went his separate way." That may be true, but it seems doubtful that anyone will ever be able to prove it. However, Lieutenant Reinhold Jahnow, who had been flying since April 1911, may have been the first German pilot to die in the war while on operations. He fell over Malmedy, Belgium, on August 12, but it is not clear whether he died as a result of gunfire from the ground or malfunction of his plane.

The first contingents of the Royal Flying Corps were flown from England to France just nine days after the Germans started their thrust through Belgium. This was the first mass movement of airplanes in history, though later one of the pilots involved, R.J.F. Barton, wrote, "I really do not think that the pilots of the Expeditionary Force had any feeling that the fly-over *en masse* was a historic event. It was just one big excitement to us."

The first R.F.C. aircraft were flown from Dover in England to Amiens in France. The first of these to land was a B.E.2 with Lieutenant H.D. Harvey-Kelley, of No. 2 Squadron, in the pilot's seat. The flight from Dover was started at 6:25 A.M., and Harvey-Kelley reached Amiens at 8:20.

In addition to No. 2 Squadron, three other squadrons plus an Aircraft Park were dispatched to France. Aircraft Park was the name given to the aviation supply and repair sections. No. 2 and No. 4 Squadrons consisted of B.E.2's, No. 3 had Blériot monoplanes and Farmans, and No. 5 was a mixture of Farmans, Avros, and B.E.8's.

Not all the planes that set out on that historic flight landed safely at their destination. One crashed during take-off, and Lieutenant R.R. Skene as well as his passenger, Air Mechanic R.K. Barlow, were killed. The records state that various crashes reduced the number, but there are no specific details. The historian of the day wrote, "At least five pilots and other personnel were killed and twice that number of aeroplanes were lost in the operation." However, it is known that Lieutenant R.M. Vaughn made a forced landing near Boulogne, where he was arrested by the French police and imprisoned for about a week for making an unauthorized flight over French soil.

That night and the next the gallant British airmen huddled together against haystacks in an effort to keep warm, for no

The Avro 504 was one of the first British planes to reach France after the outbreak of hostilities. The machine was used initially as a bomber, and later for training. *"Flight"*

A Farman S.11 Shorthorn at a front-line French airfield. This picture was taken early in the war, before guns were added. A Farman was the first Allied plane to fall to enemy fire.

provisions had been made to accommodate them. They were just there; the Royal Flying Corps of the British Expeditionary Force had arrived—and no one could have cared less!

The comedy of errors continued with the arrival of the Aircraft Park. The British commander in Amiens didn't know the outfit was coming and didn't know what to do with it or its members. In fact, he sent a message to headquarters stating, "An unnumbered unit without aeroplanes which calls itself an Aircraft Park has arrived. What are we to do with it?"

The R.F.C. crews in France thought they would be able to set up a permanent base, but this was not yet to be the case. On August 16, the Allied infantry started to retreat from Mons in the face of an overwhelming enemy onslaught, and the R.F.C. was ordered to pack its goods so it could move hastily to the rear. During the aerial retreat to Maubeuge, two more British planes crashed.

So far, the aerial weapon had not been employed with important results by either side. This was about to change. And ironically, it was the Royal Flying Corps, the only expeditionary force, which brought about the change.

The British pilots had been instructed that they were the eyes of the Army. Aside from a few isolated experiments, the British had not considered using the airplane for anything other than reconnaissance. While the ground forces were retreating from Mons, the R.F.C. took to the air on August 19 for its first reconnaissance missions. There were two flights, one a failure, the other an outstanding success.

The pilots, flying without observers, were ordered to stay together so that if one was forced to land, the other could report its location. However, on the first of these missions the planes became separated. One of the pilots flew over Brussels but failed to recognize it, became lost, landed, asked directions, and finally returned to his base with no information of value. The second pilot landed twice to ask directions, and he also returned with no information.

The second flight was more successful, and one of the pilots returned with some startling intelligence. The Germans were attempting to outflank the British infantry forces. If they had been successful, the retreat would have developed into a rout or even possible destruction of the entire British Expeditionary Force. And if this had happened, the Germans would have been able to march straight to Paris with little or no opposition. It could have meant the end of the war, almost before it had started.

Field Marshal Sir John French, commander of the British forces in France, decided to act upon this information and ordered a general retreat across the Marne River. In acknowledgment, French wrote as follows in his official dispatch:

> I wish particularly to bring to your Lordships' notice the admirable work done by the Royal Flying Corps. Their skill, energy, and perseverance have been beyond all praise. They have furnished me with the most complete and accurate information which has been of incalculable value in the conduct of operations. Fired at constantly by both friend and foe, and not hesitating to fly in every kind of weather, they have remained undaunted throughout.

August 30 was the first recorded date of use of the airplane as an offensive weapon by either side. On that day a German airplane flown by Lieutenant Franz von Hiddessen appeared over Paris and dropped four small bombs, killing one civilian and wounding four others. The people were not particularly upset by the casualties, but they were annoyed by the message the pilot also dropped: "The German army is at the gates of Paris. There is nothing for you to do but surrender. Lieutenant v. Hiddessen."

There was confusion over the type of airplane used in the attack. The French called it a Taube, but Hiddessen may have been flying an Aviatik. In those days few people could tell one airplane from another. Every German airplane in the beginning was referred to as a Taube by most ground observers, just as later virtually all single-seat fighters were erroneously called Fokkers.

A Rumpler Taube was the first airplane to be used as an offensive weapon when it dropped four small bombs on Paris. Lieutenant Franz von Hiddessen was the pilot.   *National Archives*

Several other aircraft raids were made against Paris, but none of these inflicted heavy casualties or caused anything except minor damage. One plane arrived over the city at approximately 5 P.M. on several occasions, and it was referred to as the "Five o'clock Taube."

Within a few weeks the Royal Flying Corps was again to show its value, this time in spotting for British artillery. Lieutenants D.S. Lewis and B.T. James of No. 4 Squadron were sent up in a B.E.2 equipped with a wireless set and instructions to locate three hidden enemy artillery batteries that were causing heavy casualties. Flying at almost treetop level, they finally found the batteries. After nine Morse-code messages had been sent back in thirty-five minutes, the German batteries were silenced by British guns.

The airplane was proving itself slowly, but while the war correspondent for the London *Morning Post* acknowledged its value for reconnaissance, he felt that it would eventually have other duties. "Most certainly," he wrote, "it will be challenged to fight for its information, and must be armed and equipped to accept the challenge. And where will such arming be likely to lead us? Surely to the provision of a fleet whose primary objective must be the discovery and destruction of the enemy's aircraft."

Around this time Lieutenant Louis Strange of No. 5 Squadron became the first known Allied pilot to mount a machine gun on his plane. He and his comrades had carried rifles and pistols aloft with them, taking potshots at German planes whenever they had an opportunity, but no steps had been taken to add armament as standard equipment. Strange thought he would change this, and he devised a crude mount for a Lewis gun in his observer's cockpit. Lieutenant Strange had an opportunity to test his device on August 22—though with unexpected results.

A Rumpler Taube appeared over the R.F.C. base at Maubeuge and dropped several small bombs, all of which fell short of their mark. The British flyers were ordered into the air to chase the German away with a few rifle shots, and Lieutenant Strange and his observer, Lieutenant Penn Gaskell, took off in their Henri Farman. But Strange and Gaskell had not counted on what the weight of the gun and ammunition would do to the performance of their flying machine. The Taube had been flying at an altitude of approximately 4,000 feet. The records indicate that "half an hour after it had departed the Henri Farman which had ascended to fight it was still climbing in solemn circles at 1,500 feet above the aerodrome." This was the opinion of ground observers. However, Strange himself claimed that he managed to reach a height of 3,000 feet. But the exact altitude does not matter, since the Taube had long since vanished.

After this episode, the squadron commanding officer ordered Strange to remove the Lewis gun from his airplane. "Machine guns are for the infantry," he added. "You may carry rifles with you if you wish, but nothing heavier than that."

The same orders did not apply to the French pilots. They were instructed not to take off without some sort of missile to drop on the enemy: small bombs, hand grenades, or *fléchettes* —small steel darts about the length of a pencil. *Fléchettes* were designed for use against enemy aircraft. The theory was that a French pilot could fly over a German plane, drop its load of darts, and put the enemy out of action either by injuring the pilot or damaging his machine. However, it was soon discovered that they were ineffective. There was a story circulating in the early days of the war that a German officer wearing a steel helmet and riding a horse had been hit by a *fléchette*, and that it had not only passed completely through the helmet, the man's body, and the horse, but had then buried itself three feet in the ground. The story was false. There is not one recorded instance of *fléchettes* ever causing serious injury, though they may have been responsible for some superficial wounds.

Two other air-to-air weapons tried by the French, again with no recorded effective results, were bags of bricks and grappling hooks. There were many experiments, most of them comical by today's standards and also useless.

While the warring air forces were still trying to develop their flying machines and discover what they could and could not do in military operations, many strange things were happening. The British were being fired on by their own troops as often as by the enemy. One pilot later reflected, "Up till then we had only been fired on by the French and Germans whenever we flew. Now we were fired on by the British infantry as well. I can still remember the roar of musketry that greeted two of our machines as they crossed the main road along which a British column was proceeding."

At times the fire from below was deadly accurate. The first R.F.C. crew member known to be wounded by his own forces was Sergeant-Major D.S. Jillings. A short time later another Britisher received a painful bullet wound through the seat of his pants. Immediately after this incident all the stove lids disappeared from the R.F.C. field kitchens, to be used as armor on the seats of the British pilots and observers!

Until this time, the British had been flying without national markings on their planes. In an effort to ward off fire from friendly troops, it was decided that the R.F.C. aircraft would carry identifying symbols. The first idea was to paint the British flag on the undersurfaces of the wings. But this was not good enough, because under certain lighting conditions the bars of the Union Jack looked like the German cross. In October 1914, after a pilot and his observer were killed by their own ground forces, a version of the French cockade was adopted as the official British badge.

Meanwhile, the French and German pilots and observers were also carrying pistols and rifles into combat. Two Frenchmen, Sergeant Frantz and Adjutant Quenault, scored the first Allied air victory by gunfire. On October 5, 1914, flying a Voisin, they brought down a German Aviatik with rifle fire. However, the first nonviolent victory had been scored on August 26 by Sergeant-Major Street of the R.F.C., who forced a Taube to land merely by outmaneuvering the German pilot and threatening midair collision. The names of the Germans involved in this "battle" are unknown, since they escaped after setting their Taube afire to prevent it from falling into enemy hands.

Three weeks after the R.F.C. had arrived in France, the first contingents of the Royal Naval Air Service flew across the Channel to begin operations. This was a relief to the pilots, for as Wing Commander C.R. Samson said later, "Everybody was suffering from the fear that the war would be over before we would get a chance to take part." What the R.N.A.S. air crews did not know was that they were being sent for something far more important than mere operational duties in support of the ground troops. A secret telegram to the French Ministry of Marine stated, "The [British] Admiralty consider it extremely important to deny the use of territory within one hundred miles of Dunkirk to German Zeppelins." The Royal Naval Air Service was to attack the German airship sheds, so that the huge gasbags could not be sent on bombing missions against London and other British cities.

The first of these raids was attempted on September 22 from an advance base set up at Antwerp. The objectives were the airship stations at Düsseldorf and Cologne. Two planes were sent out to each target, in miserable flying weather. Neither of these reached the objective, and one of the pilots, Lieutenant L.H. Collett, reported, "Looking for the sheds at Düsseldorf was like going into a dark room to look for a black cat who wasn't there."

A second attack was immediately planned with two planes —the first of the Sopwith Tabloids to reach France. Squadron Commander Spencer Grey was to bomb the shed at Cologne, while Flight Lieutenant R.L.G. Marix went after the installation at Düsseldorf. Grey was unable to find his target and dropped his twenty-pound bombs, instead, on the Cologne railroad station. However, Marix found the Zeppelin shed at

Düsseldorf and hit it squarely with his bombs from an altitude of 600 feet. Immediately there was a huge explosion, which demolished the shed. Later reports indicated that the newly completed Zeppelin L-9 had been inside and that its hydrogen tanks exploded, sending flames to an altitude of 500 feet. The explosion and ensuing fire reduced the shed as well as the Zeppelin to ashes. This was probably the most severe blow that aviation had delivered up to that time in the war.

There was also a considerable amount of activity on the other side of the battle lines. The Germans had organized Battle Squadron No. 1, which was known more familiarly as the *Brieftauben Abteilung Ostende,* or Ostend Carrier Pigeons. This squadron was commanded by Baron von Gerstoff, and its roster contained the names of several flyers who were later to become famous. Among these was Baron Manfred von Richthofen, who joined the unit in August 1915 as an observer.

The Ostend Carrier Pigeons had been established to fulfill a German goal to bomb England. At that time the German armies were advancing relentlessly, and when they took Calais, the Carrier Pigeons were to follow, set up a base, and operate from there to carry the war across the Channel to England. The object was to force Britain to hold troops at home for defense duties.

The Carrier Pigeons' plans were not realized, since the Germans never reached Calais. However, on the night of January 28, 1915, Gerstoff and his men swept down on Dunkirk fourteen strong, scoring three important firsts: they flew in formation, and at night, and in the first squadron-strength bombing mission.

Air action during the first five months of the war had been considerably less than impressive, but the major powers had seen enough to realize that their attitudes toward the airplane had been wrong. It was clear that if the war continued, the flying machine would become increasingly important. And so where in the past development of airplanes had been slow, it suddenly accelerated.

Fourteen German Albatros C-1's made the first squadron-strength bombing mission when they attacked Dunkirk on the night of January 28, 1915. *German Official*

Before the end of 1914, designers were at work on more dependable airplanes which could carry heavier military payloads. One of these new planes was the French Nieuport Type 10, which was designed by Gustave Delage and produced by the Société des Établissements Nieuport. The trim two-seat biplane was referred to as a "scout," but in those days the word had a different meaning from what it was to take on later. It had already been seen that the slow two-seat observation planes required replacement by machines that could fly faster and maneuver better. The Nieuport Type 10 was designed with these purposes in mind.

Two versions of the Type 10 were produced: the 10 AV, with the pilot in the rear and the observer in front of him; and the 10 AR, with the observer behind. The plane had the lines which were to become the classic Nieuport configuration, though with improvement and alteration. At first only pistols or rifles were carried by the crew, but later two machine guns were mounted—one firing to the rear, and the other firing forward over the propeller arc. Guns were mounted only in the 10 AR version, with the gunner-observer operating each—the rearward-firing weapon while sitting in his cockpit, and the forward while standing.

The Type 10 was the first in a long line of Nieuport V-strut aircraft. While the machine was generally referred to as a biplane, it was actually a sesquiplane, since the lower wing was very small and narrow and was little more than a support to brace the main top plane. It also had the structural weakness of so many Nieuports, and while one pilot wrote that it "climbed like a witch," it was notorious for breaking up in the air during violent maneuvers.

With the 80-horsepower Gnome rotary, the Type 10 had a maximum speed of 87 miles per hour. Some of the ships were modified to single-seaters and armed with either a Hotchkiss or Lewis gun mounted on the top wing, fixed to fire clear of the propeller arc. An improved, slightly enlarged version, the Type

12, mounted the 110-horsepower Clerget engine and could speed along at 98 miles per hour.

Between the Nieuport Types 10 and 12 was the Type 11 single-seater, which was basically similar in general design, and with the same structural weakness. Generally known as the *Bébé*, or Baby, the Type 11 had the 80-horsepower Gnome or Le Rhone engine and could do 97 miles per hour. The *Bébé's* wing span was about a foot and a half less than that of the Type 10 and its fuselage four feet shorter. The *Bébé* remained in front-line service through the first half of 1916 as one of the best single-seaters in the French Air Force.

Two other French planes, which first flew during the latter part of 1914 and which remained in active service for a long time, were the Voisin Type 8 pusher and the ugly but efficient twin-engined Caudron G-4.

The Caudron was used for observation purposes and as a day or night bomber. It carried a crew of two in the nacelle between the wings. Though its maximum speed was only 82 miles per hour and it required thirty-three minutes to reach 10,000 feet, the Caudron was looked upon affectionately by its crews. The machine remained in service until the spring of 1917.

The Voisin 8 also was used in daily operations until 1917. Like the Caudron, the Voisin was a two-seater, but it mounted only one engine. Maximum speed of this cumbersome bird was 62 miles per hour.

During this period the British went back to work on their S.E. design, among others. They had seen what the Sopwith Tabloid was capable of doing, and the S.E. design seemed to offer even greater potentials. The S.E.2 Bullet, which had developed from the original B.S.1, was flown in France by No. 3 Squadron, and many valuable lessons had been learned.

The next development was the S.E.4 (the S.E.3 was never built). The same basic airframe was fitted with the 140-horsepower fourteen-cylinder Gnome rotary. This remarkable airplane was years ahead of its time and was the fastest airplane

The British S.E.4 was far ahead of its time. The world's fastest airplane when it was built, it had a maximum speed of 135 miles per hour. The plane could climb 1,600 feet per minute.

Like the S.E.4, the Bristol Scout was also an advanced concept. The first models to arrive in France were unarmed, though some pilots carried pistols or rifles on patrol. *"Flight"*

flying in any country, with a maximum speed of 135 miles per hour and a climbing rate of 1,600 feet per minute.

The S.E.4 had many revolutionary features: wing flaps, a molded plastic cockpit hood, a fully cowled air-cooled engine with four-bladed propeller, and a cantilever landing gear. An interesting point about the flaps was that by an ingenious control mechanism they also acted as normal ailerons. When depressed together as flaps they extended the entire length of both wings.

Germany had also sent her designers back to work. One of the new types of planes was the Aviatik C-1, which was produced by the Automobile and Aviatik-Werke. While there was nothing spectacular or truly different in the design, the Aviatik could be relied upon to carry out its duties without falling apart or making unscheduled landings. It had the 160-horsepower Mercedes engine, which was perhaps the most reliable power plant in the world at that time, and it could do 89 miles per hour.

Another solid German machine produced during this period was the L.V.G. B-2, an improved version of the B-1. The plane used either the 100-horsepower Mercedes or the 110-horsepower Benz engine. While its maximum speed was a scant 65 miles per hour, it could climb to 3,400 feet in twelve minutes. After serving for many months in front-line duties, the B-2 was continued in service until the end of the war as a trainer. When it was assessed by the Inter-Allied Commission investigating the German aircraft industry after the Armistice, the B-2 was described as "an excellent machine with good performance characteristics."

While just a few months previously both sides had assumed that the war would be a short one—the Germans convinced that Paris would fall within a few weeks, and the Allies as confident that they could beat the Germans back—they were now settling down to some long-range planning. A new weapon had been discovered in the airplane, and they were rushing to improve it. But the real testing period was still ahead.

The Sky Fighters Emerge

Chapter Six

By THE BEGINNING of 1915 the war had begun to settle down to rows of opposing trenches. The French were strung out along a battle line 544 miles long, while the British in their sector were also digging in. Fragile airplanes flew above the trenches reporting concentrations of troops and spotting for artillery. It was strictly routine work, with few encounters between opposing airmen. A British pilot compared it with going daily from home to the office and back again.

Although there was little air action, the stage was being set for air war. The first planes in the Vickers Gun Bus series arrived in France in February, each with a swivel machine gun for the gunner-observer in the front of the nacelle. At first no squadron was fully equipped with these machines, since production was too slow. Instead, only one or two were attached to a unit to provide protection for other airplanes on reconnaissance missions. This was the first time that escort planes were used.

While the Gun Bus was later to earn a good reputation, it was anything but dependable in the beginning. Forced land-

The first of the Vickers Gun Bus two-seaters arrived in France in February 1915. The plane was the best flying machine then serving with the British.

ings were common until the pilots learned how to handle the tricky Gnome Monosoupape (single valve) engine. One pilot set a record by suffering fifteen forced landings in twenty-two flights!

A few airmen were also beginning to emerge for their daring. One of these was a Frenchman named Captain Happe, who became known as the "Pirate of the Skies."

Flying a Maurice Farman, Happe was a bombing specialist. Loaded with explosives, his pusher could rise no higher than 3,000 feet and was unable to execute any maneuver except a slow banking turn. Flying in this dangerously overloaded condition, Happe went out three times each day in permissible flying weather and dropped his bombs on any German targets he could locate. On January 10, 1915, he flew one mission that made history.

A German observation balloon was in the air near Nieder-Marschwiller, and the observer in the wicker basket was directing artillery fire with deadly accuracy. Captain Happe, operating without specific orders, decided to destroy the balloon. He bombed it to oblivion, and the resultant explosion damaged his own airplane so severely that he could barely limp back to his airdrome. This was the first time in the war that an observation balloon was brought down by aircraft of the other side.

Another pilot who made headlines in this period was Sergeant Eugene Gilbert, who had been a famous flyer in prewar days. Gilbert flew with only a rifle in his plane, yet on January 10, 1915, he was credited with his third victory, an Aviatik.

Still another Frenchman added to his fame early in 1915. This was Lieutenant Adolphe Pégoud, who on February 5 encountered two German Aviatiks over the lines in full view of both armies. Pégoud brought both the enemy ships to earth for the first double victory of the war. His observer did the shooting, but Pégoud's maneuvering was so excellent that only six shots from a rifle were required to bring down the Aviatiks. This was a feat unequaled in the war, but the gunner's name did not find its way into the historical records along with his pilot's.

In March 1915 the French ability for organization began to show itself in the conduct of aerial operations. Planes which had given trouble or were found unsuited for other reasons were withdrawn from operations and transferred to flying schools behind the lines. The French Air Force was then standardized on four types of machines: the Maurice Farman for reconnaissance, the Caudron for artillery spotting, the Voisin for bombing, and the Morane-Saulnier for scouting. The very latest designs from the factories were not yet available, but these were to be integrated into operational units as they were received from the factories.

The British were also learning more about how aerial operations should be conducted. In the early months of the war reconnaissance was the main consideration of the R.F.C. But on March 10, 1915, when the first British offensive was launched against the German trench system at Neuve-Chapelle, it was decided to bomb railroad facilities to support the ground operation and deny the German troops necessary supplies and reinforcements.

The first raids were failures, for too few planes were sent too far to bomb too many objectives. However, Louis Strange, now a captain, was able to drop three bombs on a troop train and put it out of action. During this attack Strange was flying at times at an altitude of only 200 feet, and at Courtrai he was fired at by a German sentry. The Captain put him out of action with a hand grenade!

No. 1 Squadron was next given the task of keeping all enemy aircraft away from the British lines so that the ground attack could come as a complete surprise. This was a difficult job, but it was done and the attack was a success.

During one bombing raid against German railroad stations, Lieutenant W. B. Rhodes-Moorhouse came down to an altitude of 300 feet to make certain of hitting the tracks. He flew through a hail of enemy fire and was seriously wounded in the abdomen, thigh, and hand. While he managed to bring his air-

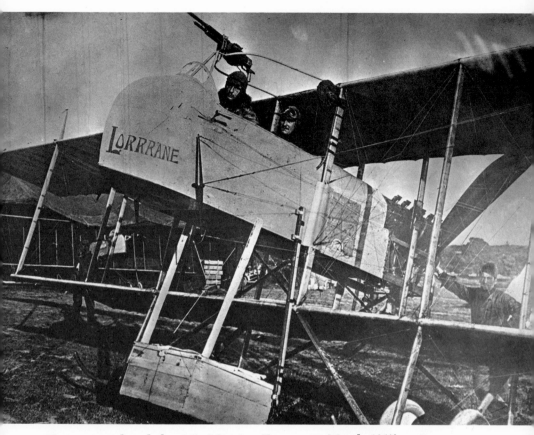

France introduced the new Maurice Farman in March 1915 as its
standard reconnaissance plane. It had a machine gun on an awk-
ward mount above the front cockpit. *U.S. Air Force*

The ugly but efficient Caudron G-4. While the machine was designed before the war, a number were still in operation as late as 1917. It was the first plane designed as a bomber.

An *escadrille* of Morane-Saulnier monoplanes at a temporary flying field. These planes carried a crew of two and were used for scouting. Top speed was 130 miles per hour.   *U.S. Air Force*

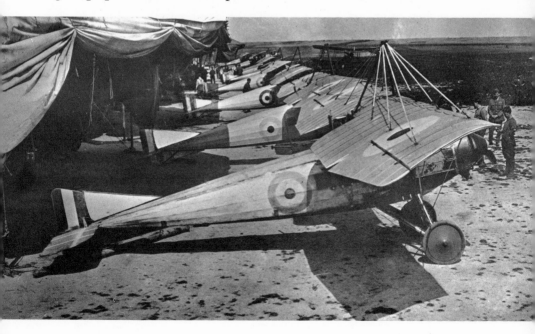

plane back safely, he died the next day. He was the first British flyer to receive the Victoria Cross, though posthumously.

Meanwhile, something radically different was happening behind the battle lines. Raymond Saulnier of the Morane-Saulnier Company had been experimenting with a system that would allow a machine gun to shoot between the revolving propeller blades. His original plan had been to synchronize the gun with the propeller, but he discarded this idea when cartridges of the Hotchkiss gun supplied to him by the French Government hung fire and caused trouble. Captain de Vergnette, commander of *Escadrille* [23], heard about the device and sent Roland Garros back to the Morane-Saulnier factory at Villacoublay to investigate. Around this same time, Eugene Gilbert, working independently and with no knowledge of the Saulnier device, thought he would be able to fire a machine gun through his propeller arc. Aware that if bullets from the gun struck the propeller it would be smashed, Gilbert wrapped the hub of each propeller blade with heavy steel wire, hoping that this would be enough to deflect the bullets.

Some have said that Gilbert first tested his device in December 1914, with a Hotchkiss gun mounted on his Morane-Saulnier Bullet, and that the following month he shot down a German plane. These claims may be correct, but they cannot be confirmed.

Raymond Saulnier's idea was similar, though with one improvement. Instead of wire, he fixed wedge-shaped pieces of steel armor plate to the hubs of the propeller blades to deflect the bullets that struck them.

Garros was enthusiastic about the device when Saulnier explained it to him. Here at last, he thought, was a means by which the airplane could be turned into a true weapon. The French would now be able to sweep the Germans from the skies. And if this happened, the Allied armies could maneuver and plan their attacks without fear of observation. The Germans would be unable to stop the offensives, and the war would be over.

The pilot's enthusiasm intensified when the tail of the Morane-Saulnier Bullet was raised and the engine started for ground tests. The stripped-down Hotchkiss on the cowling had a rate of fire of some 300 rounds per minute, though each clip held but twenty-five rounds. According to Saulnier's calculations, less than 7 percent of the bullets would strike the propeller blades. His calculations proved right, and very few bullets ricocheted from the steel wedges as Garros tested the gun on the ground.

Next came aerial tests over the field at Villacoublay, and Garros' enthusiasm increased still more. Diving at a target spread out on the ground, he hit it squarely with his bullets.

Roland Garros was anxious to try his new weapon in combat, and he flew the Morane-Saulnier back to his drome. His comrades were interested, but they were also skeptical, with the sure conviction that the constant pounding of bullets against the propeller would eventually cause it to crack and splinter. They had to be shown.

Garros showed them. On April 1 he went up to seek his first victim, whom he found in the vicinity of Ostend. One can only venture a guess about what the Germans thought as they saw the French plane maneuver to get behind them, or the reactions they had when bullets started to drill into their plane from the nose of the attacker. They were both dead when their machine hit the ground, and Garros had proved the effectiveness of his weapon.

The Frenchman scored his second and third victories on April 11, and the following afternoon he added another German to his list. By the middle of the month Garros had run his string to five victories. If his comrades had not been convinced before, they were now. Garros had demonstrated the value of his weapon, and suddenly the other pilots in his *escadrille* wanted similar planes.

That fifth victory set all Paris ablaze with enthusiasm for their aerial hero, whom they called an "ace"—meaning that he was outstanding. From that time on five victories became the standard to gain the unofficial accolade of "ace."

Roland Garros started a new chapter in aerial warfare when he flew his Morane-Saulnier Bullet into combat for the first time on April 1, 1915. Note machine gun on the fuselage.   *Peter M. Bowers*

However, Roland Garros was not long to enjoy his position as a national hero, for on April 19 his Bullet was forced down on the German side of the lines and captured intact before he was able to set fire to it. This unfortunate event was a boon to the Germans, and it was also to mark the beginning of the use of the airplane as a true weapon.

Young Anthony Fokker was called in to examine the captured plane—not because he was the most brilliant aircraft designer in Germany, but merely because his factory at Schwerin, sixty miles east of Hamburg, was producing aircraft that were little more than copies of the Morane-Saulnier. It was assumed that since Fokker had copied the airplane, he should also copy the gun arrangement. He was instructed to duplicate the device for installation on German aircraft. He was also informed that within forty-eight hours Army officials would visit his plant for demonstrations of the completed airplane.

After examining the French plane for less than an hour, Fokker was convinced that the deflector plates were not the answer. In those days aircraft engines ran about 1,200 revolutions per minute at maximum speed, which meant that a propeller blade would be in front of the gun some 2,400 times each minute. It was therefore obvious that sooner or later, no matter how good the protective armor, a blade would be shattered and the plane would be forced down.

On his way back to Schwerin, carrying a Parabellum gun and the propeller from Garros' plane, Fokker recalled how, as a schoolboy, he had thrown stones at the windmills in Holland, and how most of the stones missed the whirling blades. He wondered if it might be possible to improve upon the French device. Something far better was required, some mechanical arrangement that would prevent even one bullet from striking the propeller blades, no matter how fast or how slow the engine was running.

Fokker knew there were two ways to solve the problem mechanically. One method would be to have the fire of the machine gun interrupted whenever a propeller blade was in front of it. The other way would be to synchronize the gun by means of a cam, so that its rate of fire would actually be controlled by the propeller. He did not like the first idea, for this would cause the gun to fire erratically and might make it jam. To Fokker, it was far more practical to have a cam on the propeller shaft trip the gun only when the field of fire was clear.

Other people before Fokker had experimented with devices to allow a machine gun to shoot between the whirling blades of a propeller. In Germany alone, August Euler and Franz Schneider had tried the arrangement, Euler as early as 1910. Schneider had also produced an airplane with a synchronized gun as early as 1914. This was the L.V.G. E-6. The plane crashed while it was being flown to the front for operational assessment, and no others were built. These previous experiments were forgotten when Tony Fokker was called in to examine the captured Morane-Saulnier.

Within a period of only forty-eight hours the ingenious Fokker and his engineers devised a synchronizing gear that was practically foolproof. But proving it to the German military was another problem. "In my confidence," Fokker said later, "I had not figured on the conservative military mind, which not only has to be shown, but then wishes to be shown all over again, after which it desires a little more time to think the matter over again once more."

Fokker first demonstrated his gun arrangement on the ground, firing three bursts of ten shots each. The German Army officials examined the propeller after the engine had stopped and found it undamaged. But they were not completely sure that the device worked as Fokker claimed, and that it had not been a coincidence that the propeller blades escaped undamaged. They insisted upon an aerial demonstration.

Tony Fokker took his little E-1 *eindecker* up himself. At an altitude of 900 feet he nosed over and pointed his plane at some old wings he had laid out on the field as a target, riddling them.

The Fokker E-1 was the first airplane to have a machine gun synchronized to fire between the propeller blades. With its new weapon, the airplane suddenly became deadly.   *Peter M. Bowers*

"They [the German officers] had not foreseen that the bullets striking the stones underneath the wings would ricochet in every direction," Fokker wrote in his autobiography. "I had. When they took to their heels, running like mad to the safety of the hangars, I decided that they would never forget that the gun shot from the air as well as it did from the ground. Timidly they crept out, after I had landed, and viewed the bullet-riddled wings."

But even with this test, the officers did not realize that they had witnessed something revolutionary, a device which would transform the airplane into one of the most deadly weapons ever conceived. They contended, instead, that the only certain way to test the plane and gun was to shoot an enemy plane down.

"My protests were useless," Fokker wrote. "The official mind was made up. Without being given a choice, I found myself bundled off to the Front, and introduced to the liaison head-quarters of General von Heering, one of the Army Corps heads near Laon."

Within a short time Tony Fokker, still against his wishes, was in the air at 6,000 feet and looking for an Allied airplane on which he could test his gun. He finally located a French Farman, and he quickly got behind it and went into an attacking dive. In describing this event, the Dutchman wrote:

As the distance between us narrowed the plane grew larger in my sights. My imagination could vision my shots puncturing the gasoline tanks in front of the engine. The tank would catch fire. Even if my bullets failed to kill the pilot and observer, the ship would fall down in flames. I had my finger on the trigger. I had no personal animosity toward the French. I was flying merely to prove that a certain mechanism I had invented would work.

By this time I was near enough to open fire, and the French pilots were watching me curiously; wondering, no doubt, why I was flying up behind them. In another instant it would be all over for them.

Suddenly I decided that it was too much like "cold meat" to suit me. I had no stomach for the whole business, nor any wish to kill Frenchmen for Germans. Let them do their own killing!

After returning to the flying field from which he had taken off, Fokker announced that he was finished flying over the front. However, he agreed to show a German pilot how to operate the gun.

The first German pilot to have the Fokker with the synchonized gun was Oswald Boelcke, who had already proved himself one of the most capable military flyers, with more than sixty operational patrols over the battle lines. Boelcke had also been given credit as the pilot in Germany's first aerial victory, when he kept his observer's rifle within range of a French plane for twenty-five minutes, resulting in destruction of the enemy.

Boelcke took his new Fokker out twice in search of Allied machines, but each time he was unsuccessful. Then, on his third flight, he encountered a French plane and smashed it down with his bullets. Suddenly the German High Command realized that Anthony Fokker had indeed developed something outstanding. "From its early skepticism," the Dutch designer wrote, "Headquarters shifted to the wildest enthusiasm for the weapon."

This was the real beginning of aerial warfare. However, one plane was not enough, and Lieutenant Max Immelmann was given the second Fokker equipped with the synchronizing gear. The intrepid German took his machine into combat for the first time on August 11, 1915, while ten British B.E.'s were raiding the airdrome at Douai. Both Boelcke and Immelmann took off in the very face of bombs and climbed up after the attacking bombers. The two flyers selected British targets and went after them, machine guns blazing. However, Boelcke's Parabellum jammed after a few rounds and he was forced out of action. Undaunted, Immelmann continued the attack alone, bringing down one of the raiders piloted by Lieutenant Reid, who was only injured in the arm and lived through the remainder of the war as a prisoner.

The German High Command had envisioned the Fokker with its synchronized gun not as an offensive weapon, but only for defense of observation planes. However, Max Immelmann set the style of stalking Allied machines that crossed the lines. Immelmann and Boelcke soon worked out a plan to divide the fighting duties, with Immelman concentrating on the British while Boelcke operated against the French.

As stories about the Fokker and its forward-firing gun started to circulate on the Allied side of the lines, the pilots became apprehensive about venturing into German territory. This plane represented something against which they had no adequate defense, and the morale of the French and British airmen was shaken. In a period of four months the Germans destroyed sixty-three enemy planes against a loss of only sixteen. Very few of the sixty-three had actually been shot out of the sky by the *eindeckers,* as the records were to prove later. At the time, however, most of them were attributed to the Fokker, and the plane's reputation soared out of proportion to its actual combat performance.

Boelcke and his comrades recognized this, and they succeeded in creating an illusion of great aerial strength where no such strength existed. As a fighting force, the German airmen were outnumbered by the French and just about equal to the combined Royal Flying Corps and Royal Naval Air Service. Against this armada, the pilots with Fokkers mounting synchronized guns amounted only to six. This half-dozen gave birth to the idea of overwhelming force, invincibility, and power.

These six planes and pilots also created the legend that the Germans were cowards who would not cross their own battle lines, who dived out of the sun, struck swiftly, and then retreated to safety.

That criticism got into print and found its way to Germany, where the Fokker pilots laughed at it. Only they knew how greatly they were outnumbered and how foolish they would have been to fight against such odds. Besides, they were under strict orders not to cross the lines, for fear that one of the *eindeckers* would be forced down and fall into the hands of the enemy. The synchronizing gear had to be guarded at all costs, for it had turned the numerically inferior German Air Force into a mechanically superior force.

Among the favorite targets of the Fokker pilots were the British B.E. types, with the observer in the front cockpit. The B.E.'s were shot down in such numbers that Noel Pemberton Billing, a Member of the British Parliament, coined the phrase "Fokker Fodder" in describing the plight of the R.F.C. airmen sent out on missions against a weapon they were unable to match.

The Germans kept their synchronized gun a secret for about five months, and then one pilot, lost in a fog, landed his Fokker by mistake on a French flying field. The Germans had learned about the Garros gun by luck, and now the Allies learned about the Fokker system by the same kind of good fortune.

"The delight of the French when they found that the terrible havoc-wreaking gun which had wrought such destruction was fixed to the captured ship knew no bounds," Anthony Fokker wrote. "The ship, which was undamaged, was flown immediately to French Headquarters, we were told [by a French pilot captured soon afterward], the gun examined, and full details of its operation published in various magazines. Some French papers printed detailed drawings, more correct in fact than the drawings in my own factory because I was constantly making changes in the mechanism."

While the Germans had lost the secret of their synchronized gun, they had learned that the airplane was a far more potent weapon than they had imagined. During that year serious thought was given to future operations, and specialized duties were assigned to various classifications of aircraft. The air force was organized into four main groups: reconnaissance and observation; infantry attacks and other duties connected with ground fighting; aerial fighting, including fighter escort for machines less capable of defending themselves; and bombing, both day and night.

The first of the new airplanes under this system were delivered before the year was out. The most important of these were the Rumplers, Albatroses, and Aviatiks, all of which were improvements over previous models. As originally received by operational units, these craft had swivel Parabellum machine guns in the rear cockpit but no armament for the pilot. A fixed gun, modified from the Maxim, was later mounted on the fuselage and synchronized to fire through the propeller arc. Many of these synchronized guns were produced at the Government Arsenal at Spandau, near Berlin, and bore the name *Spandau* stamped on the casing. At the time the Allies thought this was the name of the gun, but the Germans themselves did not call any gun a Spandau. The official designation of the fixed synchronized gun was merely LMG.08 or LMG.08/15, meaning aviation model of the 1908 Maxim or the 1915 modification. The Parabellum was likewise an adaptation of the Maxim, developed by Karl Heinemann. The name *Parabellum* was Latin for "prepare for war," and derived from the saying, "If you wish for peace, prepare for war."

With the realization that aerial fighting would probably become more frequent than in the past, the gunner-observers in these new German planes were given wide fields of fire from the rear cockpits, without hampering obstructions as in the British B.E.2 and R.E.5. In the past Germany had been forced to copy and adapt because of lack of aeronautical experience. Now German engineers were beginning to lead the way with original designs, some of which would soon prove their value in combat.

In an effort to meet the challenge of the synchronized-gun Fokker, the British went to work on a single-seater which appeared to be little more than a scaled down, cleaned up version of the F.E.2 two-seater. Actually, there were two versions of this same basic design. One of these was the D.H.2 designed by Geoffrey de Havilland for the Aircraft Manufacturing Company, generally known as Airco; the other was the F.E.8 designed by J. Kenworthy of the Royal Aircraft Factory.

A comparison of the designs indicates that they were similar in layout and general performance.

The first of these, the D.H.2, had a 100-horsepower Gnome engine and a maximum speed of 93 miles per hour. Climbing time to 5,000 feet was eight and a half minutes.

The D.H.2 carried a single stripped-down Lewis gun in the nose. At first this gun was on a swivel, so it would have a larger field of fire. However, it became apparent that the pilot literally had his hands full if he tried to maneuver his plane and swivel the gun at the same time, and the gun was then mounted in the fixed position.

The F.E.8 had a slightly longer span than the D.H.2 but its length was shorter, and its loaded weight was about 100 pounds less. With the same Gnome 100-horsepower engine, it could do 94 miles per hour and was able to climb to 5,000 feet in seven minutes and twenty seconds.

While these machines were much alike, the D.H.2 later became famous as the finest single-seat pusher fighter of the war, while the F.E.8, which was delayed in going into squadron service, was already obsolete when it started its fighting career.

In France, the Nieuport biplanes were hurried into production to meet the menace of the Fokker. While the Nieuports had better performance characteristics than the German monoplane, the armament arrangement at first was hardly desirable. The Nieuport 10 had been designed as a two-seater, but it was often flown as a single-seater because of its low engine power. On July 3, 1915, Captain Brocard, who later commanded the famous Stork Squadron, shot down a German with a pistol from his Nieuport 10!

The Nieuport 11 *Bébé* was far better as a fighting machine. Not only was it faster, but the gun arrangement on the upper wing made it a dangerous adversary in skilled hands. Despite its many drawbacks, including notoriously weak wings, the Nieuport 11 helped to offset the temporary advantage of the Fokkers. French success with this machine was so impressive

In an effort to combat the Fokker menace, the British produced the D.H.2 in 1915. The plane was the best single-seat pusher fighter to see action.

that the *Bébé* was ordered by the British for the Royal Naval Air Service. It was also built in Italy by Nieuport-Macchi as the standard Italian fighter, and some models even found their way into the Russian Air Force.

As 1915 drew to a close and fighting became a regular duty of the airplane, it was obvious that the year had been one of German victory, with the Allies rushing to catch up. In the last three months of the year, the numerically superior French flyers brought down only fifteen German planes while losing twelve of their own. This was a far different situation from the one that had existed in the beginning of the year, when the Allies had had things pretty much their own way. And the German aerial onslaught had not yet started. Interference and bungling by government officials still plagued the air services, but very few leaders on either side continued to doubt that the men who flew would play an important part in the struggle.

Airpower Becomes Reality

Chapter Seven

THE YEAR 1916 opened quietly, with the opposing armies dug in on the ground in an elaborate system of trenches stretching for hundreds of miles, and with the winter proving to be a powerful foe to both sides. But warplanes continued to fly whenever the weather permitted. It was brutally cold at high altitude in the open, unheated cockpits. One British pilot wrote in his diary, "I did not care whether I was shot down or not. I was so utterly frozen that every second was an agony, with my eyeballs and everything else about me feeling like blocks of ice. There were times, in fact, when I almost wished a forward-firing Fokker would come by and rescue me with one of its bullets. It would have been almost the humane thing to do, I thought."

The aerial observers did not expect to see much of importance on either side, for this was not the kind of weather in which to launch an offensive. The ground war had been reduced to artillery duels, small patrols, desultory attrition in the trenches, and preparation for the coming spring. More than anything else, it was a struggle for the opposing armies to keep warm. Men were still dying on the ground in large numbers, but the frightful losses of the previous fall had been slashed.

The Fokker monoplane was still the most effective fighting machine in the air, even though severely limited in numbers. For some reason, the Germans had not yet ordered all of the existing planes to be fitted with synchronized guns. The original E-1 had been superseded by the improved E-2, but only twenty-three of these were built before further alterations were made and the designation changed to E-3.

Despite the numerical inferiority of the German Air Force, it continued to hold virtually uncontested control of the air. As example of the amount of respect it demanded, one single British B.E.2 sent out on reconnaissance early in the year was accompanied by no less than twelve escort machines!

Bombers continued to be the true backbone of the offensive French aerial operations. Not only did they strike regularly and effectively, but they proved to be tough adversaries.

The Caudron G-4, the first twin-engined bomber of the war, had started to display its effectiveness in the latter part of 1915. During the early months of 1916 the pilots became bolder still, aiming their attacks at targets farther behind the lines.

On January 23 a squadron of Caudrons dropped 130 bombs on the railroad station and German barracks at Metz. During the return flight they were attacked by ten Fokkers and Aviatik scouts. While the German planes were armed with synchronized machine guns against the Caudrons mounting swivel guns in the front cockpits, only one of the French machines was shot down. This success in beating off the Germans was due mostly to the fact that the Allies had now started to fly in formation for mutual protection. Encounters like this were soon to bring about specialized fighter tactics for attack against specific types of aircraft.

The bombers held the spotlight on the Allied side in the early part of the year. They dropped 252 bombs in January and accounted for three of the four enemy aircraft destroyed during that month. During the same period the Germans shot down twenty Allied planes.

In recognition of the importance of the Fokker menace, Major General Hugh Trenchard, who had taken over command of the Royal Flying Corps, issued an order on January 14, 1916, which read in part as follows:

> Until the Royal Flying Corps is in possession of a machine as good as, or better than, the German Fokker, it seems that a change in policy and tactics has become necessary. In order to ensure that reconnaissance and photography patrols are allowed a fair chance of success, all fighter aircraft will raid prominent enemy aerodromes and attack any hostile machine that offers combat.

The implication of this order was obvious. In an effort to prevent the slow, virtually defenseless observation planes from being blasted out of the sky in wholesale numbers, the fighters were to offer themselves as bait. They were to engage the Germans not only in an attempt to shoot them down, but to prevent them from turning their guns on the intelligence-gathering aircraft.

At the same time, the German Air Force had been charged with the responsibility of keeping the air clear of Allied observation planes, for the General Staff had devised a daring plan. All military strategists knew that the dead of winter was no time to launch an offensive. There were many historical examples to prove that such foolhardiness generally ended in disaster. On the assumption that they might be able to effect a surprise, the German generals decided to ignore the grim lessons of history with a huge push. The objective was to be Verdun.

Verdun was not only the key to Paris, it was the most strongly fortified town in the east of France. The Germans had previously captured it in 1870, during the Franco-Prussian War, after a siege of six weeks. If it could be captured again, Germany had hopes of a speedy victory and the end of a war that had already lasted longer than they had anticipated. But

This D.H.2, a casualty to German marksmanship or engine trouble, barely made it to a friendly trench. Note that the plane was stripped of its engine and machine gun. *Royal Canadian Air Force*

the attack had to come as a surprise if success was to be realized, and the German Air Force was given the responsibility of keeping the air around and behind Verdun clear of Allied aircraft so that troop movements and other preparations would not be observed. One hundred and sixty-eight German aircraft (most of them unarmed or carrying only swivel guns) fourteen balloons, and four dirigibles were given the task of maintaining an "aerial barrage" in the area from dawn to dusk.

The German airmen knew that the concept of the aerial barrage was foolish with such a small number of planes, and that it would be impossible to patrol at all levels. If an enemy came over at an extremely high altitude, Fokkers at a considerably lower level would not be able to climb rapidly enough to intercept them. Or if the defensive aircraft maintained patrol at an altitude near their service ceiling, there was every likelihood that an Allied plane would be able to hedgehop over the lines, slipping in and out again undetected.

The Germans struck at Verdun on February 21, 1916, with a nine-hour artillery barrage that was called the most intense in the history of warfare. Following this barrage, the German troops surged out of their trenches. The French could not withstand the onslaught, and they fell back slowly to prepared positions, taking a heavy toll of the enemy as well as losing many men themselves.

The twenty Fokkers with synchronized guns flew above this battlefield, striking at Allied aircraft while their artillery-spotting planes relayed information to the big guns below. Airmen who were later to be among the most famous in the German Air Force were in the two-seaters at Verdun. Ernst Udet and Hermann Goering were observers, while Manfred von Richthofen and Bruno Loerzer were pilots on the lumbering birds.

The artillery-spotters directed the ground guns with such accuracy that Fort Douaumont, Malancourt, and Fort Vaux, among others, were reduced to ruins. Parisian newspapers told part of the grim story:

A series of photographs of the fort at Vaux shows with what terrific weight the German artillery bore upon this work. The successive pictures are more like microscopic slides of some terrible skin disease than photographs of skillfully and strongly constructed fortifications. The whole area inside the fort, seen from a height of 4,000 feet, even before the last days of unremitting bombardment, resembles a relief map of Switzerland. On the hills and woods north and west of the position, the guns fired, not in batteries, but almost wheel against wheel. Aerial observers, unable to mark the positions of so many guns, had to content themselves with indicating the artillery regions.

The French were desperate, and they mustered the best of their air force behind the fortress. Verdun would surely fall unless the German aerial supremacy was broken. Colonel Barès was given command of all French aerial activities in the area, and he ordered that its strength be increased. When the German attack started, there were 144 French airplanes in the sector. Under Colonel Barès, this was increased to 261, including nine fighter *escadrilles*.

Every French plane that could carry a bomb was sent out again and again, and there were so many that the few Fokkers could not cope with them. "They were sending out as many as twelve fighter planes to protect two observation machines," Oswald Boelcke wrote. "It was seldom that we could get through this protecting screen to reach the observation planes." But they did get through often enough, and French losses mounted.

Then the French had a brilliant idea. Instead of concentrating on the Verdun sector, where the Germans were fairly strong in the air, they decided to launch a general assault on the enemy in other sectors. Following this plan, they dropped bombs and shot at every target they could find: troop concentrations, columns of reinforcements, supply lines, even field kitchens.

This strategy had the desired effect. There was a roar from the German infantry, a bitter cry for protection from the continuous aerial assault. A demand went out for cover, and a phrase was coined that was heard as far back as Berlin: "Gott strafe England, France, and our Air Force!" And the German General Staff made the blunder that the French had hoped they would make. They issued an order to all the squadrons that Allied aircraft were to be stopped, wherever they were. The German airmen protested that this would be foolish, that they should remain at Verdun until the job there had been completed. But the General Staff would not be swayed, and the order stood.

The Fokker pilots were so bitter over their new assignment that they tore after the French with renewed fury. In five days Boelcke alone blasted four enemy aircraft from the sky. But the Frenchmen continued to come, willing to take their chances to destroy German aerial superiority over Verdun. They were successful. The German infantry made further advances, but the prying eyes above Verdun were gone, and German casualties climbed while those of the French fell. Verdun held, and the entire course of the war was changed.

This was the first time that aviation had been used, if not actually to win a battle, then to prevent possible defeat. For there is little doubt that Verdun would have fallen under the incessant pounding from German guns if Germany had held the air secure in that sector. As it was, some 350,000 French troops and 330,000 Germans were killed in the titanic battle.

By this time, the Germans were beginning to encounter stiff opposition from the new Allied planes. Jean Navarre was cutting a flaming swath with his Nieuport *Bébé*, and Georges Guynemer and Charles Nungesser were not far behind. Added to this deadly trio were Jean Chaput, Albert Heurtaux, and Noel de Rochefort, who had become aces with five victories apiece. On the British front, the De Havilland D.H.2 had arrived, and Lanoe Hawker and other pilots of No. 24 Squadron were making their presence felt.

Both the Nieuport and the D.H.2 were superior to the Fokker monoplanes, and Anthony Fokker quickly made modifications on his original design and replaced the engine with a new

Oberursel rated at 160 horsepower, boosting the top speed to 100 miles per hour. Oswald Boelcke was sent back to the Fokker factory at Schwerin to test one of the new planes, and while it seemed to perform well, there was considerable trouble with the fourteen-cylinder, twin-row engine. He next tried the machine in combat, and was unimpressed. In his official report on the machine, Boelcke wrote:

(a) Speed of the 160-horsepower Fokker E-plane is sufficient in level flght. Climbing it loses speed so that repeatedly Nieuports escape.

(b) Ability to climb over 3,000 meters [9,843 feet] is insufficient. This may be avoided by a biplane design.

(c) Ability to turn is much less than on the 80-horsepower or 100-horsepower types. Quick turns are impossible without stopping the engine. At this one loses height, so that in combat it could prove very dangerous.

(d) Performance of the 160-horsepower engine was good at first, except that it lost power at height. After use in service, engines lost more than 100 revolutions per minute.

(e) Machine guns work well under good maintenance. Workmanship and materials used in the new design cause various troubles.

(f) Installation of the fifteen-degree upward-firing machine gun is useless. It would be preferable to use the old installation with machine guns firing in the direction of flight.

Apparently as a result of that report, Fokker went to work on his D-1. While this was a biplane and used the stationary Mercedes engine rather than the rotary Oberursal, the general design was little more than the *eindecker* with wing and engine changes, plus minor fuselage alterations to adapt it to the new engine.

Another new German airplane that started to come into service around this time was the Halberstadt D-2. The first example of this basic design, the D-1, appeared in small quantities late in 1915, and the pilots who flew it into combat reported that it was a fine machine in all respects. Built by the Halberstadter Flugzeugwerke, originally a branch of the Brit-

Last version of the Fokker *eindecker* was the E-4, which had two machine guns and a 160-horsepower engine. The plane was not as successful as earlier versions. *Peter M. Bowers*

The Halberstadt D-2 started to come into service early in 1916.
Though a single-seater, the plane was first used for reconnaissance.
Synchronized guns were added later.

ish and Colonial Aeroplane Company of Bristol, the D-2 performed so well it rarely appeared on Allied victory listings. While it had a maximum speed of only 90 miles per hour with the 120-horsepower Mercedes engine, it was highly maneuverable and strong enough to sustain long, steep dives. James Mc-Cudden, the British ace, once wrote of a Halberstadt, "I have never in my experience seen a machine, under control, dive so steeply and so long."

These excellent single-seaters were finally replaced in most front-line units with improved aircraft, but a few continued to fly until the end of the war. In May 1917, French ace Charles Nungesser was forced down by a Halberstadt. As he approached for a landing, out of ammunition, Nungesser expected to be shot down by the German on his tail. However, the enemy pilot merely flew past and waved in salute.

During this period something new and different started to take place on the German side of the lines. Boelcke had suggested that instead of fighting singly or in pairs, the Fokker, Halberstadt, and other single-seaters be formed into *jagdstaffels*, or hunting packs. Rather than escorting observation planes and bombers, the purpose of these units would be to hunt for and drive enemy aircraft and balloons from the sky. Each flight would go out in formation, following a respected leader who would inspire confidence in his followers. This was a new concept in aerial warfare and one that was to be the foundation for the later "circuses." To Boelcke's pleasure, and probably amazement, the plan was approved by General Ernst von Hoeppner, who had assumed command of the German Air Force.

Meanwhile, developments were being made rapidly in England. While the Airco Company was concentrating on producing D.H.2's as rapidly as possible, a new design had come from the Sopwith Aviation Company. This plane was built for the Royal Naval Air Service under the designation Type 9400 Two-Seater. However, it became better known as the 1½-Strutter, since the center-section cabane struts attaching the upper wing to the fuselage appeared to be composed of one and a half struts. These were actually two separate strut arrangements, but the bracing looked strange at the time, hence the strange name for the plane.

The 1½-Strutter passed its official acceptance tests on December 12, 1915, but because of bureaucratic interference it was not placed in immediate production. The Sopwith two-seater was the first British airplane to go into action with a synchronized Vickers machine gun for the pilot; the observer-gunner had a single Lewis gun on a special mounting that had been developed by Warrant Officer F.W. Scarff. With this ring mounting, the gunner sat on a stool in the middle of his cockpit and could maneuver his gun to shoot in any direction.

Performance of the 1½-Strutter was excellent. With a 110-horsepower Clerget engine, it had a maximum speed of 106 miles per hour and was able to climb to 10,000 feet in just slightly over twenty minutes.

The first Sopwith 1½-Strutters went into service with the R.N.A.S. in April 1916, and the Royal Flying Corps received its first deliveries the following month. The only reason the machine got into service this early was because the Royal Naval Air Service ordered it into production before official permission was received. When this outstanding design first appeared in combat, however, it was wearing French colors rather than British, for the French saw the original test model in December 1915, liked it, and arranged for its production in their own factories. Sopwith built 1,520 1½-Strutters for the R.N.A.S. and R.F.C., but 4,500 were produced by the French.

With the coming of better weather in the spring of 1916, fighting in the air became heavier, and the day of casual combat and routine flying were gone. By the end of May, Boelcke had eighteen victories—a greater number than any other pilot in the war. Immelmann was close behind, with fifteen, and new names were beginning to appear on the German honor roll. The Germans also flew in flights rather than going out singly, and a

The Sopwith 1½-Strutter was the first British airplane with a synchronized machine gun for the pilot. A swivel gun was also installed in the rear cockpit.

While the British F.E.2b appeared to be ungainly, it was actually a good fighting machine. An F.E.2b gunner was credited with shooting down Max Immelmann on June 18, 1916.

Imperial War Museum

few of the improved Halberstadt single-seaters now joined the Fokkers.

Then, suddenly, the German Air Force received a heavy blow. On June 17 Gerstoff, the original leader of the Ostend Carrier Pigeons, was shot down in flames. Max Immelmann was killed the following day.

The truth concerning Immelmann's death will never be known. According to the British, he was shot down by Corporal J.H. Waller, the gunner-observer in an F.E.2b piloted by Lieutenant George McCubbin. However, the official German version is that he was brought down by antiaircraft fire. Another version, by a pilot who was in Immelmann's flight that day, is that the ace shot off his own propeller, as he had on a previous occasion when something went wrong with the synchronizing gear. Boelcke's statement added further confusion. He wrote, "Immelmann lost his life through silly chance. All that has been written about a fight in the air is foolishness. A bit of his propeller flew off; the jarring tore the bracing wires connected to the fuselage and then broke away."

Regardless of the true story, Immelmann's death was a severe blow to the Germans. He had been a national hero and had been called invincible in combat. Suddenly there was doubt in the minds of the people. If Immelmann could be destroyed, their other airmen had no chance at all. It was a time of great gloom, not only for the German Air Force but for the entire country.

Boelcke and Immelmann had been fighting rivals, yet they were close friends. Boelcke vowed to avenge his comrade, and he flew even longer hours. One story is that his next victim was Victor Chapman, of the *Lafayette Escadrille,* the first American to die in the air war. However, this, like Immelmann's death, also became a controversy, with his flying mates insisting that Chapman was brought down in a general melée with five German planes. Two days later the *Lafayette Escadrille* was notified through official channels that Chapman had been promoted to sergeant and had also been nominated for the *Croix de Guerre.*

Le Prieur rockets on the wing struts of a Nieuport scout. Eight rockets were carried and were fired electrically. These weapons were used against German observation balloons.

No matter who killed Chapman, it is a fact that the German General Staff was concerned about the lowered morale of their airmen and decided to transfer Boelcke away from the Western Front. He was actually forbidden by an Imperial Decree to fly. This decree was obviously issued in fear of the cumulative effect if he should follow Immelmann in death.

Boelcke left his *staffel* on July 4. That same day ninety reinforcement aircraft arrived at the front. Of these, twenty-four were single-seat fighters and the remainder were two-seaters for reconnaissance, artillery spotting, and bombing. The German Air Force was still so short of aircraft that it continued to think in terms of defensive operations.

On the other side of the lines, aircraft were being produced in such quantities that more Americans were being encouraged to join the *Lafayette Escadrille,* the original name of which had been *Escadrille Américaine.* Activated on April 17, 1916, it was initially composed of seven Americans who had volunteered to fly for the French as a token thanks for the assistance given to the United States during the War of Independence by the Marquis Marie Joseph de Lafayette. Before the war ended, the original seven had grown to 180.

At this time, in an effort to relieve the French, who were still struggling at Verdun, the British started a massive drive through the Somme salient. As originally planned, the French were to have contributed forty divisions of infantry to this offensive. However, their losses at Verdun had been so great that they could support the British with only sixteen divisions. Because of this, the drive was largely a British operation.

The Germans met this attack with the largest concentration of airpower they had been able to muster against the British to that time—129 planes, only nineteen of which were single-seaters. The Royal Flying Corps, due to the foresight of General Trenchard, had 185 aircraft in this same area (total strength of the R.F.C. in France at that time was 421 airplanes distributed in twenty-seven squadrons), while approximately 200 more were attached to the French divisions operating with the British.

Nieuport fighters of the *Lafayette Escadrille* during the Battle of the Somme. The unit was originally composed of seven Americans who had volunteered to fly for the French.　　　*U.S. Air Force*

The German airmen were doomed from the beginning of the attack, which started on July 1. While some two million Allied troops charged forward on the ground, the Nieuports, D.H.2's, and 1½-Strutters assumed virtually unchallenged command of the air. The Fokkers and Halberstadts and few Albatros D-1's were badly outnumbered and outgunned and were forced to fight defensively, avoiding contact with the enemy fighters whenever possible so that they could conserve their strength for use against the observation planes and bombers. But these slower two-seaters were no longer the easy prey they had been in the past, for many of them now had synchronized guns up front and swivel guns in the rear cockpits.

Writing about the Battle of the Somme, the official German historian said:

> Numerous captive balloons aided observation and directed [enemy] artillery fire. Innumerable airmen with the latest machines crossed far into the rear of the German combat area. They directed their batteries, dropped bombs on troop shelters, machine-gunned batteries and marching columns and photographed the slightest details of the German defensive system. World history was witnessing the first great organized employment of aerial squadrons.

Even more graphic were the comments of the German infantrymen in the trenches. One wrote in his diary, "During the day one hardly dares to be seen in the trench, owing to the English aeroplanes. They fly so low that it is a wonder they do not pull one out of the trenches."

In an effort to improve the situation, the Germans sent all available aviation sections to the area, increasing their total strength to 299. However, the greatest number that they had available for duty on any single day was 251. At the same time, the Allies were able to put 500 aircraft into the air.

"The aerial superiority of the enemy is still complete," a German memorandum from the front stated. "It is a characteristic sign of the Somme campaign and influences all battle actions in a decisive manner."

A new phase had developed. The Fokker E-1 supremacy was gone. And where the British and French had learned their lesson and had rushed new and better machines into production to meet the challenge, with the awareness that control of the air was necessary for control of the ground, the Germans had not been sufficiently farsighted to keep pace.

But a dramatic new change was coming, and soon.

The Game Grows Deadly

Chapter Eight

ABOUT SEVEN WEEKS before the Battle of the Somme began, a young man named Albert Ball was transferred from the R.F.C.'s No. 13 Squadron to No. 11 Squadron. In his original posting Ball had flown the slow, badly outmoded B.E.2c two-seater but had also managed a little practice in a Bristol Scout single-seater. When he was transferred to No. 11 Squadron, he carried a note with him from his previous commanding officer stating that he was qualified to fly a Nieuport single-seater.

To Ball, an airplane was almost an extension of his own body, and he flew with effortless skill. He took immediately to the Nieuport, and on May 22, 1916, he scored his first two victories, neither of which was confirmed. On June 25 he shot down a German observation balloon, and this went into the records as his first confirmed victory. A week later he destroyed his first German airplane, a Roland two-seater.

Ball was given a leave from combat flying, and on August 10 he returned to No. 11 Squadron. Six days later he attacked five Germans and vanquished three of them. After another five days, when he had just turned twenty years old, he was involved in a patrol that became almost legendary. For this action he was awarded the Distinguished Service Order, with the following citation:

A Roland C-2 was the first enemy plane to fall to Albert Ball's guns. The Roland was an advanced design concept, but it mounted only one machine gun. Maximum speed was 103 miles per hour.

For conspicuous gallantry and skill. Observing seven enemy machines in formation, he immediately attacked one of them and shot it down at fifteen yards range. The remaining machines retired. Immediately afterwards, seeing five more hostile machines, he attacked one at about ten yards range and shot it down, flames coming out of the fuselage. He then attacked another of the machines, which had been firing at him, and shot it down into a village, where it landed on the top of a house. He then went to the nearest aerodrome for more ammunition, and, returning, attacked three more machines, causing them to dive under control. Being then short of petrol he came home. His own machine was badly shot about in these fights.

While the official citations merely recounted events, an American journalist named Laurence Driggs, who knew Ball, gave this account in 1917:

He dashed out in all kinds of weather, forcing a fight wherever possible and by preference fighting alone. When he sighted an enemy he darted into the attack with the ferocity of a maddened eagle. He would throw himself into the midst of a compact enemy formation and break it up through their sheer fear of collision.

Whether the opposing formation consisted of ten, fifteen, or twenty enemy aeroplanes this young hornet appeared equally indifferent. Like a Lilliputian he struck this way and that, darting with the suddenness of a serpent at an unsuspecting enemy, keeping always a wary eye, and alert as a fox, always evading at the last instant the furious assault of an enemy.

While this account sounds like the rambling of a fiction writer, it is not. Ball was foolhardy and impetuous. His favorite method of attack was to plunge headlong into an enemy formation, regardless of odds, trusting that the enemy pilots and gunners would be unable to fire at him with any accuracy for fear of hitting their own squadron-mates. Ball had more than his share of courage, but he was also one of the worst air-combat tacticians of the war. It was because of this boldness that he was able to achieve such outstanding success.

While Ball, Hawker, McCudden, and other British pilots were racking up victories on the Somme Front, the Germans were so hard pressed for fighting aircraft that they could rarely launch an offensive patrol. This forced them to fight a defensive battle.

On July 30, in an effort to placate the ground troops, who complained that they never saw one of their own airplanes flying overhead, the German Air Force organized an offensive mission and crossed the lines twenty-five strong, to strike at British targets of opportunity. However, this motley collection of airplanes was not up to the task of meeting the Nieuports, 1½-Strutters, and D.H.2's, and they were driven back before they could do any real damage.

On another occasion, a flight of ten German two-seaters was forced to jettison its bombs and flee when attacked by a patrol of three D.H.2's. The Germans had their backs to the wall in the air fighting, and they could not take unnecessary chances.

Around this time Field Marshal Paul von Hindenburg succeeded Erich von Falkenhayn as the German Chief of Staff. One of Hindenburg's first acts was to strengthen the position of his air force. Within a month, with a shift of planes from the French to British fronts, plus the fact that rush orders were placed for new fighting equipment, the German airmen regained some of their old spirit and prestige.

Another Hindenburg reform was to give General von Hoeppner, Chief of the German Air Force, more power to reorganize and equip his squadrons. Hoeppner passed part of this responsibility along to General Hermann von der Leith-Thomsen, his Chief of Staff, who had been one of the most avid German airpower advocates since 1911. These moves were to result in events which the Royal Flying Corps had not anticipated.

During this period Anthony Fokker was still attempting to produce a biplane fighter that would have wide acceptance, but none of these was outstanding. Fokker's last effort in 1916 was the D-5, which used the 100-horsepower Oberursel rotary engine. The plane was ordered into production, but it was difficult to fly and was unpopular with pilots. However, a truly outstanding single-seater had been developed by the Albatros-

Werke at Johannisthal. This was the D-1, which was one of the most graceful and advanced airplanes built in any country up to that time. Conceived by a design team headed by Robert Thelen, this sleek biplane had a plywood-covered fuselage and wooden-framework wings covered with fabric. With either the 160-horsepower Mercedes or 150-horsepower Benz, it had a maximum speed of 109 miles per hour and a service ceiling of 17,000 feet.

While the Albatros D-1 was not exceptionally fast and its climbing speed was actually less than that of the Fokker D-5, it was very strong, could be dived for long distances without fear of the wings coming off, and was the most maneuverable airplane that had ever been produced in Germany. It was also the first fighter on either side to carry two machine guns synchronized to fire through the propeller. Twin guns had previously been fitted experimentally to the Fokker *eindeckers,* and one plane had been produced for Max Immelmann with three guns. But these arrangements had not proved practical, because the extra weight of the guns and ammunition resulted in too much performance loss. The Albatros D-1, with its more powerful engine and better design, was able to carry the extra armament without sacrificing performance. James McCudden, the British ace, later testified to the firepower of the Albatros when he returned from patrol in his D.H.2 and discovered twenty-four bullet hits in his machine.

The German airmen received the Albatros D-1 with enthusiasm, but there was one complaint. In the original D-1, the center-section cabane struts were of the inverted-V type, and these obstructed forward vision. Conventional N-struts were installed to correct the difficulty, and the machine was continued in production as the D-2.

Oswald Boelcke had been concentrating on the development of his *jagdstaffel,* most of the pilots for which he had carefully selected himself. His first recruits for *Jagdstaffel 2* included Manfred von Richthofen, Werner Voss, Max Mueller, Erwin Boehme, Franz Hoehe, and Karl Immelmann, a cousin of the

The Albatros D-2 was such an excellent fighter that it quickly dominated Allied opposition. It was the first plane with twin machine guns as standard equipment. *U.S. Air Force*

Oswald Boelcke (*left*) and Werner Voss. Boelcke was Germany's foremost aerial tactician, and Voss was credited with 48 confirmed combat victories.

late Max Immelmann. These six, along with Boelcke, accounted for more than 245 confirmed victories before the war was fought to a close.

Jasta 2, as the unit became known, was officially organized on August 27, 1916, but it did not have even one airplane. The first three machines arrived on September 1—one Albatros D-1 and two new Fokkers. The following day Boelcke took the Albatros into combat for the first time and shot down a D.H.2 for his twentieth victory. Five more victories in the week of September 8–15 helped to restore confidence in the German Air Force.

Boelcke trained his fledgling pilots carefully while waiting for their airplanes to arrive, teaching them methods of attack he had worked out, instructing them where and how to approach certain Allied aircraft with the least danger to themselves. He knew that virtually every airplane had at least one blind spot, an area where its guns could not be brought into action. Boelcke was the first true aerial tactician, and he drilled the principles he had learned into his students.

The Albatros D-1's and D-2's arrived at Cambrai on September 16, and the remainder of that day was spent flying around the drome and testing the guns in the air as well as on the ground. Some sources also claim that one unidentified member of the *jasta* scored a victory that afternoon. That evening Boelcke gathered his pilots and announced that he would lead a flight into action the following morning.

Jasta 2 took off five strong with the first rays of the sun on September 17. Before they left the ground, Boelcke repeated his instructions to his eager charges, warning them to fly and fight cautiously.

Since July 1, when the Battle of the Somme was launched, the British airmen had had things pretty much their own way. They had hit 300 targets with 17,600 bombs and had scored heavily against enemy airmen. With this single patrol in the new airplanes, and with new fighting tactics, the Germans were about to demonstrate that Allied mastery of the air was at an end.

Shortly after the Albatros single-seaters took off they encountered a group of eight British B.E. bombers and six escorting F.E.2b's. Boelcke was the first of the Germans to locate the enemy machines, and he maneuvered his flight so that the Royal Flying Corps pilots could not return to their own lines without fighting.

Jasta 2 dived to the attack, and the F.E.2b's turned to give battle. But nothing could stop the Germans, and each of them scored a victory. Only the timely arrival of R.F.C. No. 60 Squadron, flying Nieuport fighters, saved the remainder of the British formation from what surely would have been a slaughter.

That day was the beginning of a new way of life for Manfred von Richthofen. He had previously flown as a gunner-observer, and had scored an unconfirmed victory, according to his story, against a French Farman two-seater during the Champagne battle in 1915. In October of that year Richthofen was given home leave, and during the train ride he accidentally met Oswald Boelcke, who at that time had scored four victories. After talking with Boelcke, Richthofen decided that he had to become a pilot, and that eventually he must fly single-seaters.

Richthofen passed his flight examinations on December 25, 1915, and in March of the following year he was sent to join the Second Battle Squadron at Verdun. But he was not content to act merely as a chauffeur for his gunner, and he had a machine gun attached to his plane—apparently on the upper wing, but Richthofen did not explain fully in his autobiography. On April 25 he shot down a Nieuport scout with this gun, though again the victory was not confirmed. The Germans did not credit enemy aircraft destroyed if they fell into Allied territory without reliable witnesses.

In June Richthofen was transferred to the Russian Front, where he flew a bomber. Here he met Boelcke the second time and was surprised when the famous ace asked him to join the fighting unit he was then in the process of forming.

When *Jasta* 2 flew out for the first time on September 17, Richthofen's ambition had finally been realized. He was in a single-seater, on the Western Front, and with the greatest of all German leaders. That day, he also scored his first confirmed victory. The pilot of the British plane he brought down was Lieutenant L. B. Morris; Lieutenant T. Rees was in the rear cockpit.

Describing the combat, Richthofen wrote:

The Englishman nearest to me was traveling in a large boat painted with dark colors. I did not reflect very long but took aim and shot. He also fired and so did I, and both of us missed our aim. A struggle began and the great point for me was to get to the rear of the fellow because I could only shoot forward with my guns. He was differently placed for his machine gun was movable. It could fire in all directions. . . .

My Englishman twisted and turned, going criss-cross. I did not think for a moment that the hostile squadron contained other Englishmen who conceivably might come to the aid of their comrade. I was animated by a single thought: "The man in front of me must come down, whatever happens."

At last a favorable moment arrived. My opponent had apparently lost sight of me. Instead of twisting and turning he flew straight along. In a fraction of a second I was at his back with my excellent machine. I gave a short series of shots with my machine guns. I had gone so close that I was afraid I might dash into the Englishman.

Suddenly, I nearly yelled with joy for the propeller of the enemy machine had stopped turning. I had shot his engine to pieces; the enemy was compelled to land, for it was impossible for him to reach his own lines. The English machine was curiously swinging to and fro. Probably something had happened to the pilot. The observer was no longer visible. Obviously I had hit the observer and he had fallen from his seat.

The Englishman landed close to the flying ground of one of our squadrons. I was so excited that I landed also and my eagerness was so great that I nearly smashed up my machine. I rushed to the English machine and saw that a lot of soldiers were running towards my enemy. When I arrived I saw that my assumption had been correct. I had shot the engine to pieces and both the pilot and the observer were severely wounded. The observer died at once and the pilot while being transported to the nearest dressing station. I honored the fallen enemy by placing a stone on his beautiful grave.

That day, September 17, the British suffered their greatest loss of the war up until that time: nine of their planes shot out of the air, while they had scored but four victories. The official British historian wrote about *Jasta 2*:

Their success, against seasoned opponents, achieved on aeroplanes which had only arrived the previous evening, constituted a remarkable performance. It gave Boelcke's new fighting squadron immediate prestige.

However, this was only the beginning of the carnage. The *Jasta 2* pilots were supreme on their section of the front. Within a period of only five weeks Oswald Boelcke ran his score from twenty to forty. During this same period his flight members accounted for another twenty British planes, six of which fell to Manfred von Richthofen's guns. Once again the morale of the Allied airmen was shaken, for they were faced with a weapon vastly superior to those they possessed.

The situation was so critical for the British that on September 30 Field Marshal Sir Douglas Haig wrote to the War Office in London and urgently requested more fighting airplanes. In partial reply to this request, one squadron of Royal Naval Air Service fighters was withdrawn from the Dunkirk area and sent to the Somme Front. This was No. 8 Squadron, which was composed of three flights: one of Nieuports, and one each of Sopwith 1½-Strutters and the new Pups. Within a short time the squadron was equipped entirely with the Sopwith Pup single-seaters. By October 23 the R.N.A.S. pilots distinguished themselves by shooting down eight enemy aircraft as well as a balloon.

Richthofen wrote that there were frequently "really big"

battles in the air, sometimes with as many as forty to sixty English machines. These odds were bound to take their toll. On September 26 Kurt Wintgens, one of the original Fokker E-1 pilots, was shot down by Albert Ball in a D.H.2. That same day Max von Mulzer, who had scored ten victories, crashed to his death while testing an Albatros D-1. Just before taking off on his last flight Mulzer was quoted as having said, "The next turn is mine. Immelmann is dead, [Otto] Parschau is dead, Wintgens is dead. I am the next in line."

The worst was yet to come for the Germans, for the greatest tragedy struck while they were enjoying aerial victory.

On October 28, Oswald Boelcke led five of his pilots on patrol. They encountered two British D.H.2's, and Boelcke gave the signal to attack. The British planes were from No. 24 Squadron, and they were piloted by Lieutenants A.E. McKay and A.G. Knight.

Richthofen wrote in his diary:

We were six and they were two. If they had been twenty and if Boelcke had given us the signal to attack we should not have been at all surprised.

The struggle began in the usual way. Boelcke tackled the one and I the other. I had to let go because one of the German machines got in my way. I looked around and noticed Boelcke settling his victim about 200 yards away from me.

It was the usual thing. Boelcke would shoot down his opponent and I had to look on. Close to Boelcke flew a good friend of his. It was an interesting struggle. Both men were shooting. It was probable that the Englishman would fall at any moment.

Suddenly I noticed an unnatural movement of the two German machines. Immediately I thought: Collision. I had not yet seen a collision in the air. I had imagined that it would look quite different. In reality, what happened was not a collision. The two machines merely touched one another. However, if two machines go at the tremendous pace of flying machines, the slightest contact has the effect of a violent concussion.

Boelcke drew away from his victim and descended in large curves. He did not seem to be falling, but when I saw him descending below me I noticed that part of his planes had broken off. I could not see what happened afterwards, but in the clouds he lost an entire plane. Now his machine was no longer steerable. It fell, accompanied all the time by Boelcke's faithful friend.

It is interesting that neither Richthofen nor any of the other *Jasta* 2 pilots ever identified the other pilot in the collision. However, it later became known that this was Erwin Boehme, Boelcke's star pupil and one of his closest friends. Boehme was so disturbed by the tragedy that he attempted suicide, but was restrained by his fellow pilots. It was difficult to live with the thought that he had killed the idol of all Germany, the man who had seemed to be invincible in combat.

Boelcke was twenty-four years old when he died.

Germany was shaken by this tragedy, but at the front life went on as usual. Lieutenant Stephan Kirmaier was appointed to succeed Boelcke, and by Imperial Decree the name of *Jasta* 2 was changed to *Jasta Boelcke*. Under its new leadership, the *jasta* scored twenty-five victories in the following month, but it also suffered casualties, one of which was its new commander. The leadership was then passed on to Captain Franz Walz.

While the Germans were saddened by Boelcke's death, the British soon felt a grievous loss of their own. On November 23 Major Lanoe Hawker, the Royal Flying Corps' first ace, was shot from the sky by Manfred von Richthofen. Hawker had reached his twenty-sixth birthday, which was old for a fighter pilot.

Flying his Albatros on a solo patrol, Richthofen encountered three D.H.2's in the vicinity of Bapaume. While the German ace was at 10,000 feet, the British were at a higher altitude. Richthofen waited for one of the R.F.C. planes to come after him. His wait was not long, for shortly Hawker came down in a dive. The battle that followed was one of the epic aerial duels of the war, and it took place in sight of British as well as German trenches. The story of what happened was best told by Richthofen himself:

The Englishman tried to catch me up in the rear while I tried to get behind him. So we circled round and round like madmen after one another.

First we circled twenty times to the left, and then thirty to the right. Each tried to get behind and above the other.

Soon I discovered that I was not meeting a beginner. He had not the slightest intention of breaking off the fight. He was traveling in a machine which turned beautifully. However, my own was better at rising than his, and I succeeded at last in getting above and beyond my English waltzing partner.

The sky duel continued down to 6,000 feet, and then to 3,000, with neither gaining an advantage. For some reason the two other British planes did not join the fight, and Hawker and Richthofen kept at it completely alone, each a master at the controls, each flying with skill and finesse.

Richthofen wrote:

My Englishman was a good sportsman, but by and by the thing became a little too hot for him. He had to decide whether he would land on German ground or whether he would fly back to the English lines. Of course he tried the latter, after having endeavored in vain to escape me by loopings and such like tricks. At that time his first bullets were flying around me, for hitherto neither of us had been able to do any shooting.

When he had come down to about 300 feet he tried to escape by flying in a zig-zag course during which, as is well known, it is difficult for an observer to shoot. That was my most favorable moment. I followed him to an altitude of from 250 to 150 feet, firing all the time. The Englishman could not help falling. But the jamming of my guns nearly robbed me of my success.

My opponent fell, shot through the head, 150 feet behind our lines. His machine gun was dug out of the ground and it ornaments the entrance of my dwelling.

The fall of 1916 was the high point of the German aerial effort until that time, and the lowest for the Allies. In September the Allies (mostly British) lost 123 aircraft over the Somme while German casualties were twenty-seven. The following month eighty-eight Allied planes went down while the Germans lost only twelve, and in November 104 Allied planes fell.

This destruction was wrought by the Germans with a numerically inferior air force. At the high point in the Battle of the Somme there were 333 aircraft wearing the black cross, while the British had 378 and the French about 375. North of the Somme area to Dunkirk the British were nearly double the strength of the German units that opposed them.

According to official records, the four bitter months of the Somme battle cost Britain the lives of 867 airmen. In desperation, General Trenchard requested that the R.F.C. strength be boosted to 106 active and ninety-five reserve squadrons. At twelve aircraft to a squadron (later raised to eighteen), this would have meant a total force of 2,412 planes. Supporting his request, Trenchard wrote an official communication to the War Office:

Throughout the summer the Royal Flying Corps maintained such a measure of superiority over the enemy in the air that it was enabled to render services of incalculable value. The result is that the enemy has made extraordinary efforts to increase the number, and develop the speed and power, of his fighting machines. He has unfortunately succeeded in doing so.

Within the last few weeks the enemy has brought into action on the Somme front a considerable number of fighting aeroplanes which are faster, handier, and capable of attaining a greater height than any at my disposal with the exception of one squadron of single-seater "Nieuports," one of "F.E. Rolls-Royce," and one of "Sopwiths,"—the last mentioned being inferior to the enemy's new machines in some respects though superior in others. All other fighting machines at my disposal are decidedly inferior. The result of the advent of the enemy's improved machines has been a marked increase in the casualties suffered by the Royal Flying Corps. The situation threatens to be very serious unless adequate steps to deal with it are taken at once.

The "considerable number" of improved enemy aircraft brought into action was very few indeed. There is no exact record of the number of Albatros single-seat fighters produced, but according to official German documents captured after the war ended, in November 1916 there was a total of only fifty

D-1's and twenty-eight D-2's serving at the front. Attrition no doubt claimed others, but assuming 40 percent loss, which was the R.F.C.'s average for the war, this would have meant there were no more than a total of 124 Albatros D-1's and D-2's in operation.

Control of the air had passed on to the outnumbered Germans so completely that one entire flight of D.H.2's was destroyed while on patrol. Moreover, the Germans were so emboldened that they started their bombing attacks once again, hitting Saint-Omer, Dunkirk, Boulogne, Calais, and other locations in the British sector. In one of these raids, the Germans blew up the ammunition dump at Audruicq, destroying twenty-three sheds, 8,000 tons of ammunition, and a mile of railroad tracks.

The ascendancy of the German fighter planes allowed their two-seaters to fly over the lines again, photographing and observing for artillery. As a result, their gunfire became far more accurate, breaking up attacks that had been expected to succeed. To add further harassment, the Germans started night bombing again.

The Germans had done more than regain mastery of the air over their enemies. They had also removed the prying eyes of the R.F.C. from the gigantic battle raging on the ground. During the first four months of the Battle of the Somme the British artillery had enjoyed an overwhelming superiority, due primarily to airplane observation. The Fourth Army alone had 1,721 artillery shoots observed on German batteries, silencing, damaging, or destroying more than 800 of these. In addition, 281 shoots were observed on enemy trench systems.

After British observation planes were removed from the area of the ground battle, the character of that battle also changed. Without precise information on where to put their shells, the artillery units lost their effectiveness. Their infantry advance also halted because of lack of support, and because the enemy batteries became more accurate.

The Germans retreated to the Hindenburg Line, which had been prepared in advance, remaining there until starting their own offensive on March 21, 1918. The Allies had succeeded in taking about 125 square miles of territory, but the price had been terrible. Almost 750,000 British and French soldiers fell in battle, along with 500,000 Germans.

The Albatros fighters, along with a few Halberstadts and Rolands, had contributed to preventing an Allied break-through at the Somme, just as the Germans had been stalled at Verdun when they withdrew their airplanes from the front to fight French planes in other sectors.

The ironic aspect of all this, however, is that the British did possess an airplane that could have stopped the Albatros fight-ers. This was the Sopwith Pup, which had first appeared in February 1916. As early as May one of these outstanding air-craft flown by S.J. Goble scored its first victory. No. 8 Squadron of the Royal Naval Air Service, which was sent to support the hard-pressed R.F.C., scored twenty victories in Pups in less than two months.

The official designation of the Pup in the R.N.A.S. was Sop-with Type 9901; in the R.F.C. it was known as the Sopwith Scout. However, since it followed the 1½-Strutter and was con-siderably smaller, pilots nicknamed it the "Pup." Official circles tried to discourage this, but they were unsuccessful.

The Pup had many excellent qualities. It was small, light, delightful to fly, and was a superior fighting machine. Because of its low wing loading, it could climb higher than any other fighting plane of its day, and still remain sensitive to con-trol. Late in 1915 the 1½-Strutter set a new British altitude record when it was flown to 18,400 feet. This was beaten by a Pup, which passed the 25,000-foot level. James McCudden once wrote that "at 16,000 feet the Albatros scout began to find its ceiling just where the Pup was still speedy and maneuver-able."

Listed service ceiling of the Pup was 17,500 feet. It could

The Sopwith Pup was the only British airplane that could challenge
the German Albatros fighter. It was actually more maneuverable
at high altitude, but it had only one synchronized gun.

also climb better than the Albatros, requiring less than five and a half minutes to reach 5,000 feet. With the 80-horsepower Le Rhone rotary engine, it had a speed of 111 miles per hour at sea level and 103 at 9,000 feet. One synchronized Vickers machine gun was standard equipment.

There were at least two squadrons of Sopwith Pups in France before the end of 1916, in addition to the sixty-two 1½-Strutters that had been handed over to the Royal Flying Corps by the R.N.A.S. It is not clear why this force, along with the D.H.2's and twenty-nine Nieuport scouts which had been loaned to the R.F.C. by the R.N.A.S. in March 1916, were not enough to stop the Albatros D-1's and D-2's.

While the British were being hit so badly in the air, they did not go on the defensive but continued to press forward in spite of losses. On one occasion Major L. W. Rees in a D.H.2 attacked ten enemy bombers single-handed, breaking up the formation. Rees did not shoot down any of the Germans, but he forced them to retire to their own lines. For this action he was awarded the Victoria Cross.

The British summed up the aviation aspect of the Somme battle:

> Pilots and observers flew without rest and fought a type of warfare new to the world with the age-old spirit of their race. But if they fought with an old courage, they gave it a new meaning, bringing to it something of the buoyancy and something, too, of the restlessness of the air itself. They did not belittle their risks. Rather they accepted them as the price to be paid for the joy of the new life that was theirs. Many of the squadrons suffered grievous losses, but they came from the battle strong in the knowledge that they had been called upon to play a big part and that they had not failed.

The fact that the Germans were not truly defeated on this battlefield also had a partial effect on something else that happened before the end of 1916.

Earlier in the year President Woodrow Wilson of the United

States attempted to bring about negotiations between the fighting powers that, in his words, "would bring peace without victory" to either side. In December the Germans announced that they were willing to enter into peace negotiations. However, the British turned down the proposal, since the military situation at the time was so favorable to the Germans that "no acceptable terms could reasonably be expected."

And so the war continued, and milllions more were to die. . . .

Slaughter in the Sky

Chapter Nine

WHEN THE YEAR 1917 began, Germany was so qualitatively strong in the air on the Western Front that occasionally the British were forced to send single-seat Nieuports and Sopwith Pups on long-distance reconnaissance because the slower, less maneuverable two-seaters could not get through.

Never before, even when the Fokker E-1 was the most potent plane in the air, had the Germans felt such confidence. The Albatros D-1 and D-2 had proved themselves superior to anything the Allies had, and now the improved D-3 started to come through.

The Germans were the complete masters, despite the fact that they were still badly outnumbered. Their fighter pilots also started to patrol beyond the German trenches, and in one single month seventeen R.F.C. aircraft were brought down behind their own lines—something which had never happened before in this number.

There is little doubt that even more success would have been achieved with the Albatros fighters if a larger number of pilots had been available. There was not only a shortage of trained pilots, but a scarcity of recruits for flight training. To correct these difficulties, General von Hoeppner set higher standards for training and also organized flying demonstrations in various German cities to attract new recruits.

The first *jastas* had proved so successful that now several others were organized, with a target of thirty-seven by April. Under this reorganization, Manfred von Richthofen was given command of *Jasta 11* immediately after his sixteenth victory. Erwin Boehme was installed as commander of *Jasta Boelcke*, and Bruno Loerzer took over the leadership of *Jasta 26*.

Meanwhile, there was a considerable amount of activity on the Allied side, the full effects of which would not be felt for several months to come. Some of this change was in reorganization, but most of it was in terms of new aircraft.

In 1915 the S.P.A.D. company had produced the most outlandish airplane of the war. This was the Type A-2. Something was needed to stop the Fokkers, and the A-2 was one attempt at a solution. The airplane itself had the lines that were to become classic, except that there was no real nose and the engine was so embedded in the fuselage that an opening had to be cut in the leading edge of the upper wing so it would be clear of the propeller arc. In front of all this—including the propeller—was a nacelle for the gunner. The object had been to provide a platform that would allow forward firing from a tractor airplane. However, the entire concept was a failure, and gunners were understandably reluctant to venture off the ground in the contraption.

M. Béchereau, the chief designer for the Spad concern, used this same basic airplane, with modifications, and turned it into the S-7 single-seater, which was first flown in May 1916. This was to become one of the outstanding French fighters of the war.

The first Spad S-7's were sent to the fighting front for evaluation as early as October 1916, and the pilots gave the plane enthusiastic reports. It was not as fast as some other fighters, but it was extremely strong and would not break up or shed fabric in the steepest dives or the most violent maneuvers. It had one Vickers gun fixed to fire forward through the propeller arc.

Spad S-7's were delivered to the *Lafayette Escadrille* late in 1916. Here, Raoul Lufbery supervises the refueling of his plane. The American flag was flown at this field for the first time.

U.S. Air Force

Most famous of the Nieuport designs, the Type 17 was one of the outstanding fighters of the war. It had a top speed of 107 miles per hour and was highly maneuverable. *Peter M. Bowers*

However, the gun arrangement caused problems, for the synchronization gear was so complicated that when a jam occurred it was sometimes necessary to partially dismantle the engine. This could not be done in the air, and a pilot with a jammed gun was disarmed. Despite this problem, the Spad S-7 had an excellent combat record and was flown to fame by the Storks, the *Lafayette Escadrille,* and other French units. It was also placed in production for the British and, later, for the Americans.

The first S-7's came through with 140-horsepower Hispano-Suiza engines, but the pilots were not satisfied, insisting that more power was required. This problem was soon remedied by installation of the 180-horsepower Hispano-Suiza. With this engine the S-7 had a maximum speed of 120 miles per hour at 6,500 feet, making it the fastest fighter then flying. It also climbed well, reaching 6,500 feet in just over six and a half minutes.

During this period the Nieuport scout was improved up to the Type 17. While the first models of the 17 reached operational squadrons in March 1916 for combat evaluation, production versions did not begin to come through until the end of the year.

The Nieuport 17 was highly maneuverable and responsive to the controls, but it had the same wing weakness as other Nieuport models. This weakness was caused by the fact that there was only one spar in the lower wing, and this had a tendency to buckle under stress. "A sharp maneuver simply ripped the fabric off the airplane's wings," Captain Edward Rickenbacker wrote. "At one time or another, almost all of us who flew Nieuports were victimized by this structural weakness. It was the direct cause of the capture of Captain James Norman Hall. Some of the others, like myself, were able to walk away from the wrecks. In fact, the great Major James Meissner did so twice."

While the Nieuport 17 was similar to the earlier Type 11 *Bébé,* it was larger, more powerful, and faster. It could do 107 miles per hour at 6,500 feet with the 110-horsepower Le Rhone rotary.

Across the English Channel in Britain there was also much activity, and some of the designs that started to come from the factories were to become famous.

One of these was the Sopwith Triplane, which was one of the finest, most maneuverable aircraft ever produced. The Tripe, as it became known, was designed to fill a specific need. Combat experience with the D.H.2 and other craft proved that in fighting, maneuverability was far more important than sheer speed. Engineers also knew that, generally, the shorter the wing span, the greater the maneuverability. At the same time, a light wing loading was required. This had been one of the main reasons for the success of the Sopwith Pup. If a plane could be produced with a short span as well as a low wing loading, it would be able to turn inside of machines with longer spans and higher wing loadings.

The Tripe was Sopwith's answer, and it was a good answer. In tests, the Tripe was capable of turning inside of other British fighters. It could also climb better, roll better, and turn a tighter loop.

The Tripe had a maximum speed of 117 miles per hour at 5,000 feet with the 110-horsepower Clerget engine, and it could climb to 6,500 feet in six and a half minutes. Service ceiling was 20,500 feet, which was greater than that of any other British single-seater produced to that time, and its landing speed was a bare 35 miles per hour.

The Sopwith Triplane was to write headlines during its time at the fighting front. The first sixty production models were handed over to the R.N.A.S. in February 1917. In three months these speedy fighters accounted for no less than eighty-seven enemy craft.

Another historic British plane to appear at this time was the Airco D.H.4, designed by Geoffrey de Havilland. It was the first British airplane specifically designed for day-bombing duties, and it remained in service throughout the remainder of the war.

A flight of D.H.4's returning from a bombing mission. The plane was the finest British day bomber and had a high ceiling as well as good performance characteristics.

Until the advent of the D.H.4, day and night bombing was done with general-purpose planes—"Corps reconnaissance," as they were officially termed—or converted fighters, such as the single-seat Martinsyde G.100 Elephant and the two-seat F.E.2b.

Parallel to the development of new aircraft, the British also produced new aircraft engines. This was necessary, for the airplane builders had been forced to depend heavily upon French engines, and these did not come through rapidly enough. Of the 150 Le Rhone engines ordered for the last quarter of 1915, for example, only ten were actually delivered. One of the new British engines was the Rolls-Royce twelve-cylinder, liquid-cooled Eagle, which was one of the finest power plants ever produced. With this splendid engine, the first D.H.4's were sent to France early in 1917. Georges Constantinesco's hydraulic firing gear was also incorporated into the machine, thus synchronizing the pilot's Vickers gun to fire through the propeller arc. The Constantinesco gear was far superior to any other synchronizing method developed by the Allies until that time.

With its 250-horsepower engine, the D.H.4 had a speed of 119 miles per hour at 3,000 feet and a service ceiling of 16,000 feet. Normal bomb load consisted of two 230-pound or four 112-pound bombs.

The British had realized as early as December 1914 that if they expected to carry the air war to the German rear areas with any effect, they would have to develop a special airplane for the task. In line with this long-range plan, Commodore Murray Sueter requested that the aviation industry submit designs for a "bloody paralyzer." This request resulted in the world's first true heavy bomber, the Handley Page 0/100.

The 0/100 was taken into the air for the first time on December 17, 1915, but it was not satisfactory. The test pilot complained that the ship had a violent tail flutter, was too heavy on the controls, and that its engines were not sufficiently powerful.

The Handley Page company went about making the necessary changes, and by the time the new prototype was ready, the

Huge for its day, the Handley Page 0/400 had a wing span of 100 feet and carried a bomb load of 1,952 pounds. However, it had a maximum speed of only 85 miles per hour. *Imperial War Museum*

new Rolls-Royce Eagle engines were also available. The improved machine was rolled out as the 0/400, which was almost identical in size and layout to the original 0/100.

A huge machine for its day, the 0/400 carried a crew of four and had a normal bomb load of sixteen 112-pound bombs. While the maximum speed was only 85 miles per hour, the aerial behemoth carried up to five machine guns for defensive purposes and was thus difficult to bring down.

The stage was being set for an ever-larger battle for control of the air, but the Albatros fighters were still superior in normal operations.

The weather was miserable in France as 1917 opened, and this curtailed aerial operations. Despite the weather, some patrols were flown. On one occasion a flight of eight twin-engine Caudrons of the French Air Force went trench-strafing in the Verdun sector, operating over the German lines for an hour and a half at an altitude of less than 250 feet. Only one of the attacking planes was lost, and this fell to ground fire rather than enemy aircraft. The French also continued to go on bombing missions, dropping 11.9 tons in January and 33.5 tons in February.

When Richthofen assumed command of *Jasta 11* the group had not scored a single victory. The Baron himself accounted for the first two entries in the official log: an F.E.8 on January 23 and an F.E.2 the following day. However, Richthofen was almost killed in this latter engagement when one of the lower wings on his Albatros D-3 cracked and buckled. And while Captain O. Greig of the R.F.C. landed intact on German soil, the Albatros was wrecked when it overturned on landing.

"They were the first two Englishmen I had brought down alive," the German ace wrote in his diary. "Consequently, it gave me particular pleasure to talk to them. I asked them whether they had previously seen my machine in the air, and one of them replied, 'Oh, yes. I know your machine very well. We call it *Le Petit Rouge.*'"

Although the major German aerial effort was being directed

against the British, the French were receiving enough punishment to cause alarm. On March 14 there was a bitter session in the Chamber of Deputies in Paris, during which an enraged member shouted:

"France is proceeding on the premise that any second-rate airplane is satisfactory if it provides a Frenchman with a means of dying gloriously for his beloved country!"

This debate was spurred by a report issued by Air Minister Daniel Vincent, in which he said that while the total number of French combat aircraft at the front amounted to 1,418, only 328 of these were fighters and 253 were bombers. Adding further to the unhappy news was the fact that the majority of these were antiquated and not suited to aerial fighting.

But while there was stormy parliamentary debate in Paris, changes were being made in the operational *escadrilles*. The Storks, for one, had been equipped with the new Spad S-7's, and Georges Guynemer began to score more frequently than before. His tally sheet by the end of the month showed thirty-five confirmed victories. His closest rivals were Charles Nungesser with twenty; Alfred Heurtaux, whose record matched Nungesser's; and René Dorme, who had scored seventeen victories before being seriously wounded on December 20, 1916.

That same month the British were being hit badly. On March 9, nine R.E.8's were attacked by Richthofen and his *Jasta 11*. All of the R.F.C. machines were destroyed, and not one of the Germans was brought down. On March 24, an entire formation of five Sopwith 1½-Strutters was shot out of the air, and two days later a flight of three F.E.2b's was wiped out.

Richthofen set a blistering example for his new *jasta*, scoring ten times that month and running his total to thirty-one. Kurt Wolff, commander of *Jasta 4*, closed the month with a total score of eighteen, which matched Wilhelm Frankl's record. Behind these leaders were Kurt Allmenroeder with fifteen and Karl Schaefer with twelve. But setting an even faster pace was a young flyer named Werner Voss, who had experienced victory for the first time on November 19, 1916. Despite the bad flying weather in the first two months of 1917, Voss brought down ten British planes. By March 23 he had sixteen victories and was cited with a medal for valor. He celebrated that decoration with two more British aircraft on March 24, and then scored four more times before the month was over. He was not yet twenty years old, but he was Germany's second-ranking ace.

While the British had been in a difficult position in the fall of 1916, when the Albatros fighters first appeared, this was nothing by comparison with the problems they suffered early in 1917. Of the 120 planes they lost in March alone, fifty-nine fell behind their own lines. Despite all their efforts, the men of the R.F.C. and R.N.A.S. were being put on the defensive. The new airplanes and the new pilots were arriving, but not in sufficient numbers to make up for losses.

As bad as the situation was in the first three months of the year, this was only a prelude of what was to come in April. The British had decided to launch a huge ground campaign at Arras as their spring offensive, and it opened with an artillery bombardment surpassing even Verdun and the Somme. This operation, which history books call the Third Battle of Arras, resulted from the decision of Field Marshal Sir Douglas Haig, commander of the British forces in France, to capture Vimy Ridge preliminary to an even larger offensive against Ypres.

This was to be a gigantic battle, and the Royal Flying Corps mustered as much strength as possible to support ground operations and attempt to gain control of the air. However, only 265 airplanes could be assembled to launch the campaign. Against this force, the Germans had 195 aircraft in operational units in the same sector.

Again the Germans were outnumbered, but again they held the air. That month has gone down in the annals of the British as "Bloody April," for it was a month of slaughter unparalleled in aerial warfare, either then or later. For while there would be higher losses than in Bloody April, the percentages were never again as enormous.

A fantastic five to one ratio was scored by the Germans—five

British planes shot out of the sky for every German lost in combat. Total victory claims by German pilots that single month amounted to 368, which was more than the combined totals for the previous five months!

In part, these losses can be attributed to the British refusal to go on the defensive even while they were receiving huge injuries. They continued to bore in and to lose brave men and expensive equipment. This staunchness was a British tradition, and it had to be maintained no matter what the cost.

Bloody April opened on the 4th of the month, and by the 8th —just five days—seventy-five British planes were shot down in combat and fifty-six others were lost in accidents, many of these as a result of damage sustained from enemy guns. This came to a total of nineteen men known killed, seventy-three missing, and thirteen wounded. On April 6 alone—the day the United States declared war on Germany—no less than forty-four British planes were destroyed!

In one of these engagements, an entire flight of F.E.2d's was shot down without taking a single German plane with them. In another meeting, six Bristol Fighters of No. 48 Squadron led by Captain W. Leefe Robinson were decimated. These were the first of the Bristols to go into operation, and rather than take advantage of their maneuverability so that the pilots could also use their synchronized guns, they made the mistake of remaining in tight formation. Richthofen and four of his men engaged the "Brisfits" and shot down four of them in a battle lasting fifteen minutes—two of the British planes falling to the German leader.

Richthofen wrote about the combat in his official report: "It was a new type of plane, which we had not seen before, and it appears to be quick and rather handy, with a powerful motor, V-shaped and twelve-cylindered."

Neither the German ace nor his men realized just how quick and handy the Bristol Fighter was to prove itself. Captain Andrew McKeever was one pilot who later learned that the machine was actually a single-seater with the added advantage of

The Bristol Fighter was unsuccessful in combat until its pilots learned that the machine could be flown like a single-seater, with the advantage of a rear gunner.

a "sting in the tail." On November 30, 1917, he and his gunner scored five victories in one battle—four of them Albatros scouts. By the end of the war, McKeever had run his list up to thirty, a record unequaled by any other two-seater pilot.

All through April the carnage continued. On the 13th Richthofen and his men shot down thirteen British planes without sustaining a single casualty themselves, and on April 22 *Jasta 11*, which had been organized only in the middle of January, scored its 100th victory, thirty of which had fallen to Richthofen.

With the opening of the week beginning April 27, the business of killing in the air spurted anew. In those seven days, twenty-six British machines were shot down, all except three of them falling to pilots of *Jasta 11*. During this period, on the 29th, the man who had now earned the name "Bloody Baron" scored four times—his high point for any day in the war.

During the single month of April Richthofen shot down twenty-one Allied airplanes, which was only ten less than his total had been when the month began. But he was not the only German who had taken a high toll. His brother Lothar, who was fresh from a flying school, registered his first unconfirmed success on March 25, 1917, and by the end of April he had scored twenty times. Kurt Wolff also added eleven victims to his tally in just one week, while Karl Schaefer boosted his record to twenty-seven.

On May 1 Manfred von Richthofen was given orders to go on home leave, and his brother assumed temporary command. Four days later Lothar was shot down and severely wounded.

Meanwhile, Fate was preparing a severe blow for the Royal Flying Corps.

As far back as 1912 the British had produced the B.S.1, which was subsequently refined through the S.E.2, S.E.4, and S.E.4a through 1915. Late in 1916 a still later modification of this basic design, the S.E.5, was flown for the first time. Although the test pilot, Major Frank Gooden, was killed in this machine the following month, it was placed in immediate production. The first squadron in France to be equipped with the new machines was No. 56.

There is no doubt that the S.E.5 was a superb fighting machine. It was square and squat and had very little streamlining, but it was exceptionally strong and was one of the easiest planes to fly that had ever been produced by the Royal Aircraft Factory. The S.E.5 and its successor, the S.E.5a, were rivals of the Sopwith Camel for the title of most successful British fighter of the war. At the time of the Armistice, 5,205 of these ships had been constructed. No. 56 Squadron alone was officially credited with 427 enemy aircraft destroyed.

In its original version, the S.E.5 used a Hispano-Suiza engine of 150 horsepower, and many pilots felt that a larger engine was required. Among these was Albert Ball, who favored the Nieuport.

During that bloody month of April, No. 56 Squadron lost heavily, yet it also scored many successes with the new aircraft. On May 5 Ball shot down two Albatros scouts, bringing his score to forty-three. The following day he raised his record to forty-four. It was his last victory.

On May 7 the squadron was ordered to patrol the area between Douai and Cambrai from 6 o'clock in the morning until 10:30, and again from 6:30 P.M. until nightfall. Ball and ten of his companions went up on the dusk patrol that day, and only five returned. Among the missing was Ball himself. Cecil Lewis wrote in his classic book *Sagittarius Rising:*

The Mess was very quiet that night. The Adjutant remained in his office, hoping against hope to have news of the six missing pilots, and, later, news did come through that two had been forced down, shot in the engine, and that two others had been wounded.

But Ball never returned. I believe I was the last to see him in his red-nosed S.E. going east at 8,000 feet. He flew straight into the white face of an enormous cloud. I followed. But when I came out on the other side, he was nowhere to be seen. All next day a feeling of depression hung over the squadron. We mooned about the sheds, still hoping for news. The day after that hope was given up.

It was decided to go over to Douai and drop message-bags containing requests, written in German, for news of his fate. We crossed the lines at 13,000 feet. Douai was renowned for its anti-aircraft. They were not to know the squadron was in mourning, and made it hot for us. The flying splinters ripped the planes. Over the town the message-bags were dropped, and the formation returned without encountering a single enemy machine.

Several days later the Germans dropped the following message:

R.F.C. Captain Ball was brought down in a fight in the air on May 7, 1917, by a pilot who was of the same order as himself. He was buried at Annoeulin.

The Germans erroneously gave Lothar von Richthofen credit for defeating Ball. In all the German accounts, the younger Richthofen received confirmation of a triplane as his twenty-second victory, and that day Ball was in a biplane. In fact, No. 56 Squadron had never had any Sopwith Triplanes issued to it. But even assuming that the observers were wrong and the victory had been against an S.E.5, Manfred von Richthofen himself wrote that Lothar was in a hospital on May 7. The best guess, therefore, is that Ball fell as a result of structural failure, or because of damage sustained in the combat that took place before he crashed. The only other alternative is that he received a direct hit from an antiaircraft gun. The true story will never be known.

A month later Albert Ball, the highest-scoring Allied ace, was awarded the Victoria Cross posthumously. The citation read, in part:

For most conspicuous and consistent bravery from the 25th April to the 6th May, 1917, during which period Captain Ball took part in twenty-six combats in the air, and destroyed eleven hostile aeroplanes, drove two down out of control, and forced several others to land.

In these combats Captain Ball, flying alone, on one occasion fought six hostile machines, twice he fought five, and once four. When leading two other British aeroplanes he attacked an enemy formation of eight. On each of these occasions he brought down at least one enemy. . . .

In all, Captain Ball has destroyed forty-three German aeroplanes and one balloon, and has always displayed most exceptional courage, determination, and skill.

When Albert Ball died he was just twenty years old.

Meanwhile, the British were in for another shock, which brought the war home to the people far more than the daily headlines and lists of casualties. On May 25, 1917, German Gothas droned across the North Sea and dropped their bombs on English cities for the first time. The object of this and other such raids was to keep British aircraft pinned down for home defense. At the end of 1916 only one German airplane had got through to London—an L.V.G. piloted by Deck-Officer Pau Brandt, with Lieutenant Walther Ilges in the rear cockpit. They dropped six small bombs, which landed near Victoria Station and injured ten people. In anticipation of other such raids, and also to combat Zeppelins, 17,340 officers and men were serving in the home antiaircraft service; there were also 110 airplanes as well as some 2,200 R.F.C. personnel stationed at home flying fields. The Germans wanted to force the British to increase the defensive force in men and machines.

When the Germans realized that too many Zeppelins were being lost in attacks against England and that small aircraft could not be used effectively, they decided to build large, long-range bombers for the job. One of these was the Gotha.

Some writers have stated that the Gotha was based on the Handley Page 0/400, pointing to the fact that due to navigational error one of the first of the Handley Page machines was delivered intact to the enemy on January 1, 1917. However, the first Gotha was completed by the Gothaer Waggonfabrik plant in the fall of 1916. It appears that this was the G-2; there is no record of whether the G-1 was actually built or existed

While the German Gotha was considerably smaller than the British Handley Page 0/400, it was more successful in actual operations and had a higher ceiling.

only on paper. The Germans were impressed with the machine and ordered it into production, with a goal of thirty by February 1, 1917. Because of various delays, including design alterations, the production models were not available in number until the spring of 1917, at which time they were handed over to Heavy Bombing Squadron No. 3, commanded by Captain E. von Brandenburg.

Considerably smaller than the Handley Page bomber, the Gotha had two 260-horsepower Mercedes engines, and maximum speed was 87 miles per hour. While the 0/400 had a service ceiling of only 10,000 feet, the Gotha could reach 21,325 feet. A crew of three was carried, and normal load ranged from 660 pounds to 1,100 pounds, depending upon operational requirements.

On May 25, twenty-one Gothas took off from their bases and headed toward England at an altitude of 18,000 feet. They had planned to strike at London, but heavy clouds forced them to seek other targets. They unloaded their bombs on Shorncliffe and Folkestone, killing ninety-five people and injuring 195.

The Gothas returned to England on June 5, and again they were unable to get through to London. Eight days later the weather was perfect, and fourteen of the bombers hit the British capital. Captain Brandenburg wrote in his report:

> The Thames bridges, the railway stations, the City, even the Bank of England could be recognized. The antiaircraft fire over London was not particularly strong and was badly directed. Many enemy fighting aeroplanes had, meanwhile, nearly reached the height of the squadron. In all, sixteen enemy aircraft, which flew independently, were counted. The number which ascended may be rightly estimated as about thirty. Only one of them attacked.
>
> Our aircraft circled round and dropped their bombs with no hurry or trouble. According to our observation, a [power] station in the City, and a Thames bridge, probably Tower Bridge, were hit. Of all our bombs it can be said that the majority fell among the docks and among the City warehouses. The effect must have

been great. After the bombs had been thrown, the squadron closed formation again. The aeroplanes, lightened of the loads, flew well and the pursuing enemy aircraft gave up at the coast. All the [German] areoplanes landed safely on their aerodrome.

Captain Brandenburg was wrong in his estimate of the number of British planes sent up in an attempt to intercept the raiders. The actual number was not thirty, but ninety-two. However, he was correct in saying that only one of these attacked. This was a Bristol Fighter from No. 35 Training Squadron, and Captain C.H. Keevil, the gunner, was killed by fire from one of the Gothas.

A total of 118 bombs weighing 8,771 pounds was dropped during this raid, seventy-two of them falling during a period of only two minutes within a radius of one mile from the Liverpool railway station, and total damage was estimated at about $500,-000. In addition, 162 civilians were killed and 423 injured.

This first daylight raid on London was quickly followed by others, and the British were alarmed. They insisted upon more home protection, and at least two squadrons of fighters were withdrawn from front-line operations. One of these was No. 56, with S.E.5's, and the other was No. 66, which flew Sopwith Pups. Before the war was over, approximately 400 airplanes were stationed in England or along the English Channel in France for home-defense duties.

But even in their time of great aerial success, the German pilots were becoming uneasy. The *jastas* had fought hard and had won an overwhelming victory. At the same time, the attrition rate had been too high. The superior numbers of their enemies, plus the new planes they were meeting in combat, had begun to turn the tide.

When Courage Rode Wings

Chapter Ten

THE NEW ALLIED FIGHTERS were taking such a toll of German aircraft that the basic Albatros design was improved in an effort to keep pace. The new version was called the D-5, but comparison of the plans indicates that aside from rounding the fuselage, there was very little alteration. The wing area was increased slightly and engine output was also stepped up a few horsepower. However, general performance remained about the same. But even though the single-spar lower wing had caused problems, this was not altered and pilots were cautioned not to dive their machines too long or too steeply because of the danger of buckling.

While just a month or so previously the embattled R.F.C. had sent out as many as fifteen fighters to protect as few as three photo-reconnaissance planes, the new and better machines arriving from home factories were now giving them an edge. In the entire year of 1915 only 399 British-built airplanes were sent to France. This was increased to 1,082 in 1916, and in 1917 the supply rate was more than quadrupled. German production was also increasing, but it was only about half of the combined Allied output. Added to this was the fact that the Germans were forced to commit airplanes to four fronts: the British, French, Italian, and Russian.

In an effort to regain superiority, the Germans again reorganized their air force. Under the new plan, four *jastas* would be grouped into a *jagdgeschwader*, or fleet of hunters, consisting of forty-eight planes at full complement. The object was to provide strength for unified operations rather than individual *jasta* skirmishes. The first of these experimental hunting fleets was placed in the command of Manfred von Richthofen and was composed of *Jastas 4, 6, 10,* and *11. Jasta 4* was led by Kurt von Doering, who had three victories; *Jasta 6* was given over to Eduard Dostler, who had scored fifteen times; *Jasta 10* was commanded by Ernst von Althaus, who ended the war with nine victories; and the new commander of *Jasta 11* was Kurt Wolff, who had now run his tally to thirty. *Jagdgeschwader 1* (usually abbreviated to *J.G.1*) was placed in operation on June 26, 1917. This was actually the first of the units that the British airmen referred to as "circuses."

During the week of June 1 to 7, the Germans were badly mauled by the Royal Flying Corps. In those seven days twenty-four German planes were destroyed in the air and others were driven down out of control but not listed as confirmed victories. This destruction was a result of careful planning. The ground commanders had decided to attempt to capture the Messines Ridge directly south of Ypres, and they coordinated their aircraft and artillery to work as a team.

No single battle in the war up to this point had been launched with as much careful foresight. The British outnumbered the Germans in the air by a two-to-one ratio. With this force, they were able to work one airplane for every 400 yards of front, as compared to one for every 1,000 yards in the Battle of Arras. A total of 280 of the R.F.C. machines had wireless equipment to relay shooting information to the artillery batteries on the ground. The number of artillery pieces brought up for this engagement was stupendous, with one gun for every four and a half yards of front!

The attack began with the explosion of 400 tons of mines, which had been planted earlier, and then the artillery opened up. For a period of ten days, the British fired more than half a ton of ammunition each day for *every yard* of German trench facing them.

While this attack was in progress on the ground, R.F.C. airplanes went after enemy airdromes. They bombed and strafed the flying fields at Cambrai, Bissegem, and Recken. They attacked trains, troops being brought up, supply depots, and trenches.

Captain William Bishop, the great Canadian ace, won his Victoria Cross for one of these attacks. On June 2, flying a Nieuport 17, he set a new high for daring in a one-man attack against an enemy airdrome. He flew low over the field and raked the German airplanes with machine-gun fire just as they were being brought from the hangars. Four of the enemy machines took off to intercept him, and he brought down one of these before it had reached an altitude of 100 feet. He also got two of the remaining three while they were still climbing out. When Bishop landed at his own field, his plane was riddled with bullets. However, he had proved that surprise tactics coupled with daring could pay big dividends.

Edward Rickenbacker had nothing but praise for the Canadian ace. He once said, "Bishop was the raider, always seeking the enemy wherever he could be found. Billy Bishop was a man absolutely without fear. I think he's the only man I ever met who was incapable of fear."

The situation was bad for the Germans and rapidly becoming worse. Manfred von Richthofen's leave was canceled, since he was needed at the front. He returned to *Jasta 11* on June 14, where he discovered that Karl Schaefer, his old companion and victor in thirty aerial battles, had been killed. What he did not know was that the credit had been given to Lieutenant Erwin Rhys-Davids, who along with Bishop was one of the brightest young hunters in the revitalized Royal Flying Corps.

At this point, with larger numbers of aircraft of superior

Captain William Bishop in the cockpit of his Nieuport 17, demonstrating how his gun had to fire. Bishop was second to none for daring courage. *Royal Canadian Air Force*

quality, the R.F.C. was able to observe carefully for artillery shoots. As the battle raged on the ground, more than 700 calls for bombardment on specific targets were radioed by reconnaissance planes to artillery batteries. The Germans tried to retaliate and managed to damage many of the British guns. However, aerial observation cut short the enemy's effectiveness.

Meanwhile, the French were giving the Germans no respite. They were still concentrating on bombing, and early in June they set a two-day record for tonnage dropped. These raids were carried out with as many as twenty-five planes to a flight, and twelve different targets were hit. An official French communiqué of June 15 read:

Over fifty raids were made, mostly by night, but in some cases by day. In all, seventy tons of bombs were dropped. On the 3rd and 4th of June alone, French bombing squadrons rained down nearly thirty-seven tons of bombs on the enemy.

The Germans were forced to send airplanes to do the job that their artillery was unable to do, and they strafed British trenches and concentrated heavier attacks against observation balloons. Six captive balloons were spotting for the Second Army, and all of these were destroyed on one day.

Despite fierce opposition on the ground, the British were successful and took the Messines Ridge. But while the Germans had been pushed back, they were by no means beaten. Taking advantage of low clouds and mist that rolled in on July 8, thus grounding R.F.C. planes, the German infantry launched a counterattack and killed 3,000 British troops and 126 officers in only two days. If there had been aircraft in the area to spot, it is doubtful that the losses would have approached these figures.

Richthofen flew every day and added five more victories to his list by July 2. Four days later he was shot down and seriously wounded.

The Baron had been out with his entire *jagdgeschwader*, numbering about forty planes. Part of this hunting fleet, including Richthofen and Wolff, attacked a flight of ancient F.E.2d's. As the Germans came in, Richthofen ran into a burst of lead from the Lewis gun of Lieutenant Albert Woodbridge. A bullet slashed through his helmet and across his skull, and his plane went spinning down as he lost consciousness. The rush of air partially revived him and, almost on the ground, he pulled up and landed next to a road, with no damage to his machine. At that time he had fifty-seven victories, and this was his closest brush with death.

Even more problems were in store for the Germans. They not only had to contend with the Nieuport 17, Spad S-7 and S-13, S.E.5 and S.E.5a, and the Sopwith Triplane, but now the extraordinary Sopwith Camel was starting to appear. This plane was just the reverse of the S.E.5 in concept. For while the Royal Aircraft Factory fighter was built as a stable gun platform, the Camel was intentionally designed to be unstable, on the assumption that this would make it more maneuverable. The assumption was correct, and the Camel became the most successful single-seater put into the air by the British during the war. First shipments of the plane arrived in France in June 1917, and by the end of July two complete squadrons were in action. The Camel remained in production until the end of the war, and 5,490 were built. During its combat life it accounted for 1,294 enemy machines confirmed destroyed. Part of the success of the Camel was due to the fact that it was the first British fighter with two synchronized Vickers guns.

When this Sopwith design first came out in the winter of 1916, it was referred to as "the big Pup," but the unofficial name Camel was soon adopted. The official designation was merely Sopwith F.1. The plane's unstable characteristics made it difficult to fly, and the records show that many students crashed the first time they took a Camel into the air. However, in the hands of an experienced pilot it was an excellent airplane.

Perhaps the best description of the Camel was given by Norman MacMillan, who flew it with No. 45 Squadron. He wrote:

The S.E.5a was blunt and angular, but it was formidable in combat. The plane was fast, extremely strong, and easy to fly. The fastest model could do 137 miles per hour.   *"Flight"*

Some pilots called the Sopwith Camel a "beast" to fly, but it became the most successful British single-seater. From July 1917 until the Armistice, Camels accounted for 1,294 enemy aircraft.

The Camel was a fierce little beast. She answered readily to intelligent handling, but she was utterly remorseless against brutal or ignorant treatment. The Camel turned very swiftly to the right, a feature that was partly incidental to the big gyroscopic forces produced by the rotary engine in her light framework of wood and wire. It was mainly on this ability that she won her fame.

MacMillan failed to add that in left-hand turns the ship's nose tended to rise, while it dropped during turns to the right. A tight turn in either direction, uncorrected, often caused the plane to fall into a spin.

With the 130-horsepower Clerget engine, the Camel had a maximum speed of 115 miles per hour at 6,500 feet. And while it appeared to be larger than the Pup, its wing span was only a foot and a half more, while the fuselage length was actually some 7 inches less than that of the Pup.

At this time a considerable amount of activity was also taking place in Germany far beyond the sound of the guns. Anthony Fokker and his chief designer, Reinhold Platz, had been working on a new airplane. This eventually became the Dr.1 (Dr. was the abbreviation for *dreidecker,* or triplane). An unusual airplane in every respect, the *dreidecker* was the result of an unusual theory. Fokker wanted to produce an airplane that would be practically invincible in a fight lasting perhaps ten or fifteen minutes. At the same time, he felt that it was immaterial how long it took the machine to get to the battle or how long it required to return to its base. With these thoughts in mind, he and Platz set about designing the *dreidecker,* intentionally planning to use a high-lift wing—and even adding a small "wing" on the axle between the wheels, to realize yet more lift. No other airplane in combat could match the triplane's amazing climb. It could reach 3,280 feet in less than three minutes and 16,400 feet in only fourteen minutes and thirty seconds. By comparison, the Sopwith Tripe required twenty-six minutes and thirty seconds to climb to 16,400 feet!

Many historians of World War I have claimed that the Fokker Dr.1 was designed and built as a result of the success of the Sopwith Triplane. However, the records indicate that this is not correct. Fokker and Platz started work on the Dr.1 in the fall of 1916. This was well before the Sopwith went into combat. The first model of the Fokker, which was then called the V-3 (the V meant *Versuchsmaschine,* or experimental machine), was ready and flying before the first Sopwith was brought down intact on the German side of the lines.

Fokker and Platz had been experimenting with aircraft featuring completely cantilever wings, with no interplane bracing struts. The first of these was the V-1, a trim biplane with a welded steel-tube fuselage and plywood-çovered wings. The second was the V-2, which was actually not a new design but the V-1 with a Mercedes engine instead of an Oberursel rotary. These were both turned down by the German military. Next came the V-3, a cantilever triplane. This was also rejected, since German officials believed the machine would not be strong enough and would lose its unbraced wings in combat.

Fokker took the triplane back to his factory and added single struts between the wings. These were for appearance only and not for bracing, since they were merely lengths of thin spruce. Fokker had used welded steel tubing for cabane struts to attach the upper wing to the fuselage, and he felt that these would hold up under the normal stress and strain of combat maneuvers.

The trick worked, and the plane was ordered into production as the Dr.1. Total production amounted to only 320, the last of which was completed in May 1918.

The Fokker triplane has been called "perhaps the most maneuverable airplane built for all time." This was due to the general design plus the fact that its loaded weight was only 1,280 pounds. "You climb up a few hundred meters in the twinkling of a second," one Dr.1 pilot wrote, "and then go round and round one spot like a top." Maximum speed of the plane with a 110-horsepower Oberursel was listed at 115 miles per hour at sea level and 103 at 13,120 feet.

The Dr.1 was outclassed by several Allied fighters in speed.

Fokker's Dr.1 triplane was called "perhaps the most maneuverable airplane built for all time." This is the plane in which Manfred von Richthofen scored 21 of his 80 victories.

Anthony Fokker with one of his unsuccessful designs, the V-1
biplane. Note lack of struts between the wings. The Dr.1 was
originally produced along the same cantilever principle.

"They never had an opportunity to realize how slow the triplane was," Fokker wrote, "because of the way it climbed, flipped, and stunted in flight."

Werner Voss received one of the first three production Dr.1's on August 28, 1917, and in a period of three weeks he scored twenty-two times with it. Another of these was given to Manfred von Richthofen, and while at first he did not take to his new mount, he later wrote glowing reports about its performance. Both Voss and Richthofen were also killed while flying Fokker triplanes.

While engineers were working on their latest war machines, the men at the front were continuing their daily business of bloody death.

The Allies, and particularly the British, were unrelenting in their campaign to gain complete domination in the air, and they went out constantly in search of enemy aircraft. On July 12 there was a single dogfight in which at least sixty machines were engaged. The toll that day was fourteen Germans and nine British. By the end of the month the size of these aerial battles had grown even larger, with ninety-four single-seaters engaged in one huge twisting, zooming, and diving melée.

Whereas just a short time previously the Germans had been patroling farther and farther into Allied territory, they now remained deeper in their own territory in most cases, unwilling to lose any more of their small number of aircraft than absolutely necessary. Because of this change in tactics, some R.F.C. pilots went out solo against targets of opportunity. One such flight, made by Lieutenant R.A. Mayberry, was an outstanding example of daring.

The records indicate that Mayberry went out in his S.E.5 and "flew along a road at about thirty feet, dropped a bomb on Heule aerodrome which caused immense excitement, dropped two more bombs on two hangars, and one on Courtrai station, dived at a machine-gun and sprayed the hangars from twenty feet, at one time actually touched the ground, stampeded two horsemen, attacked a goods train, scattered a column of infantry, and shot down an enemy aircraft."

The British continued their attack in the Ypres sector, but despite aerial superiority, the operation was far short of the success they had expected. Some of this failure was because torrents of rain poured from the clouds day after day, turning the battered ground into a huge mire. They had planned to advance twenty miles but achieved only two as men, pack animals, and machines became bogged down in the sea of mud. They also encountered German concrete machine-gun emplacements, or pillboxes, for the first time. The toll of infantrymen killed and wounded was frightful.

While the Allies and the Germans were losing men on the ground, losses were also suffered in the air. One of the airmen to fall at this time was Georges Guynemer, the French ace of aces, who had become the idol of his country.

Guynemer had suffered from poor health most of his life. Making him even less likely as a candidate for heroism was the fact that he was delicate, frail, and so underweight he did not appear to have the stamina required for any kind of physical work, much less military duty. When Germany declared war on France in 1914, Guynemer tried to enlist in the army and was rejected. He next tried the navy, and again he was turned down. Undaunted, he went to an air force recruitment office on November 21, 1914. This time he was accepted, but as an apprentice mechanic. On January 26 the following year he was transferred to the flying school at Pau, and on March 10 he took an airplane up for the first time.

Guynemer was posted to *Escadrille M.S.3*, which was then under the command of Captain Brocard, and he arrived at his new base on June 8. He was given a Morane-Saulnier Parasol, and an observer named Guerder was assigned to the same ship. Guynemer's first victory came the following month, on July 19. He recorded the details in his diary:

Left [the airdrome] with Guerder after a Boche [was] reported as being over Coeuvres, catching up with him over Pierrefonds:

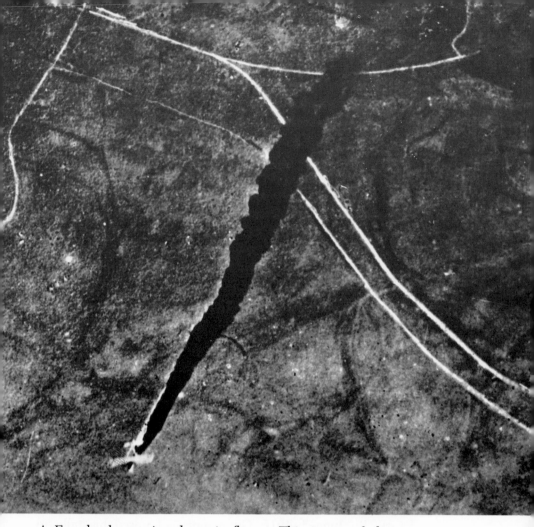

A French plane going down in flames. This is one of the most remarkable photographs of the war, since combat pictures were rarely taken by either side.   *U.S. Air Force*

fired one belt of cartridges, gun jammed, then got to working again. The Boche fled and landed near Laon. At Coucy we made a semi-circle and saw an Aviatik, at 3,200 meters, flying towards Soissons. We followed him, and when he was over our lines we dived and placed ourselves some fifty meters below him, to the rear and left. At the first volley the Aviatik lurched and we saw the flash of his fire. He was coming back at us with a rifle, and planted one bullet in a wing, and another bullet grazed Guerder's hand and head. At my last volley the pilot sank back in the fuse-lage, the observer raised his arms, and the Aviatik fell like a plummet, in flames, between the trenches.

For this feat Guynemer was awarded the *Médaille Militaire,* with the following citation:

A Pilot of great spirit and daring, willing to carry out the most dangerous assignments. After a relentless chase, brought down a German aeroplane in combat, a combat which ended in its crash-ing in flames.

Two months later Guynemer was shot down—the first of seven times. He was then flying a Nieuport *Bébé.*

By the end of 1916 Guynemer had twenty-five confirmed vic-tories. Meanwhile, his *escadrille* had adopted a name—the *Cigognes Escadrille,* or Stork Squadron—and was also trans-ferred to Nancy. And suddenly victory came quickly after victory. By June 5, 1917, Guynemer had raised his tally to forty-five. On July 6 and 7 he brought his score to forty-eight, and by August 20 it had risen to fifty-three. Some historians claim that he shot down another German on September 6, but Guynemer's own diary does not confirm this.

Then, on September 11, Guynemer took off on patrol with Lieutenant Benjamen Bozon-Verduraz. He never returned.

The Germans later reported that Guynemer had been shot down by a Lieutenant Weisemann over Poelcapelle, Belgium. One wing of his Spad had broken in the crash, and the pilot had received a bullet in his head. Neither he nor his machine were ever recovered. The area where Guynemer fell was pounded by British artillery, and all evidence of the pilot's grave and his Spad were obliterated.

Today, in Paris, in the crypt of the Pantheon, there is a plaque attached to one of the walls bearing the name Guynemer, with the following inscription:

Died on the field of honor, September 11th, 1917. A hero of legendary power fell under the open heavens of glory, after three years of hard fighting. He will long remain the purest symbol of the race. Of indomitable tenacity, boundless energy, sublime courage. Animated by a moving faith in victory, he has bequeathed to the French soldier an imperishable legacy which will raise high the spirit of sacrifice and bring forth the noblest emulation.

It took France a long time to recover from the blow of Guynemer's death. However, another hero had started to emerge, a man who had only twelve victories when Guynemer died. This was René Fonck, who eventually blazed even a greater trail in the war-torn skies.

Then, on September 15, another great airman fell, this time a German, Kurt Wolff, who was officially credited with thirty-three victories. Eight days later—September 23—Werner Voss fell in a battle that James McCudden later described as the greatest one-man show of the war.

Voss had taken over command of *Jasta 10* after returning from the quiet French Front, to which he had been transferred on April 5. He came back to the Ypres sector in the middle of August 1917. On the 20th he destroyed a Sopwith Camel. The following day he shot down an S.E.5, and the next day he scored a double victory. He finished the month with a total record of thirty-nine. Every member of his *jasta* had also scored, and without a single loss.

Meanwhile, something new was taking place on the Allied side. The British had been going out in fairly small formations, each of them scouting independently. But now they decided to patrol in concentrated force: Camels in the lead, with S.E.5's behind and higher, and then, even higher, a flight of Bristol Fighters. The plan had been worked out by the pilots themselves, and without official approval.

Despite these large battle formations, Voss continued to score heavily. Between September 6 and 12 he brought down seven R.F.C. planes, six of them Camels and S.E.5's.

On September 23, with his score at forty-seven, Voss went on a solo patrol in his Fokker Dr.1. Far below him he spotted a four-tiered battle formation of Camels, S.E.5's, and Bristol Fighters, while under these were two flights of R.E.8's. Oblivious to the odds, the German flyer dropped the nose of his triplane and dived straight at the S.E.5's. He selected one of these as his target, holding his fire until he knew he could not miss. The distance closed rapidly, and suddenly he poured a burst into it. The British plane went down, trailing smoke. This was Werner Voss' forty-eighth and final victory.

This sky battle was such a classic that it must be told in the words of those who participated or looked on as observers. First from McCudden, one of the S.E.5 pilots:

The Hun triplane was practically underneath our formation now, so we dived at colossal speed. I went to the right, Rhys-Davids to the left, and we got behind the triplane together. The German pilot turned in a most disconcertingly quick manner, not climbing nor making an Immelmann turn, but in a sort of flat, half spin. By now the German triplane was in the middle of our formation and its handling was wonderful to behold. The pilot seemed to be firing at all of us simultaneously and, although I got behind him a second time, I could hardly stay there for a second.

Major Rothesay Wortley, leader of the Bristol Fighter flight, added this:

For eight minutes on end he fought the eight [actually now seven], while I sat 1,000 feet above, watching with profoundest admiration this display of skill and daring.

The dexterity of his maneuvering was quite amazing. He was in and out and round about our scouts zigzagging like forked lightning through the sky. None of our men could get at him. Then he broke off the fight and darted off to join a Flight of Albatri [Albatros scouts] which had appeared upon the scene— and were hanging about some distance away as if hesitating to take part. Placing himself at the head of this formation, he again wheeled to the attack. But the Albatri proved themselves unworthy of their would-be leader. They followed him to just within range of our machines, and then they turned and fled.

The triplane came on alone; again he flew to the attack; but, as was bound to happen in the end, the heavy odds against him told their tale.

James McCudden refuted part of this story:

By this time, a red-nosed Albatros scout had arrived and was apparently doing its best to guard the triplane's tail. The formation of six Albatros scouts [Rhys-Davids put the number at eleven] stayed above us and were prevented from diving on us by the arrival of a formation of Spads.

The triplane was still circling around in the midst of six S.E.'s who were all firing at it as opportunity offered, and at one time I noted the triplane in the apex of a cone of tracer bullets from at least five machines simultaneously, and each machine had two guns.

When Erwin Rhys-Davids returned to his drome and handed in his combat report, it said:

I got in several good bursts at the triplane without apparent effect. Twice I placed a new Lewis drum on my gun. Eventually I got east and slightly above the triplane, and made for it, and got in a whole Lewis drum and a corresponding number of Vickers into him. He made no attempt to turn until I was so close to him that I was certain that we would collide. He passed my right hand wing by inches and went down.

Rhys-Davids was given credit for the victory, but it was James McCudden who composed the fitting epitaph to Werner Voss:

As long as I live, I shall never forget my admiration of that German pilot who single-handed fought seven of us for ten minutes and also put some bullets through all of our machines. His flying was wonderful, his courage magnificent, and, in my opinion, he was the bravest German airman whom it has been my privilege to see fight.

By this time the British had established the aerial superiority they sought. On September 23 alone, nineteen Germans were shot down and only three British planes were admitted lost. However, it was not a completely one-sided story. In the six days of the Battle at Menin Road the R.F.C. used twenty-six squadrons—468 planes at full strength—and lost sixty-two pilots and observers killed, wounded, or missing. For the entire month, the Germans claimed a total of 263 victories against the British and French.

The Germans lost two of their finest pilots in the heavy fighting. One of these was Heinrich Gontermann, who had been flying into combat since 1915 and had destroyed eighteen observation balloons and twenty-one airplanes, for a total of thirty-nine. He was killed in a flying accident on October 30, when part of the top wing of his Fokker Dr.1 broke away. Anthony Fokker had been sure that his triplane would withstand any combat maneuvers. Apparently he was wrong, as so many other aircraft designers had been.

Erwin Boehme was the next to fall. After his collision with Boelcke a year previously, he had flown recklessly, almost seeking death. He had led *Jasta* 2 to many victories, and he had scored twenty-four times himself. He was killed in action on November 29, the same day that he was awarded his *Pour le Mérite*.

The British had gained in the air, but they had not swept the Germans to defeat. Throughout the Battles of Ypres and Cambrai, the R.F.C. lost approximately 30 percent of its aircraft and personnel. In August alone the British brought down 238 enemy aircraft, while in the same period they and the French lost 263 in combat as well as others in accidents. However, the tide had been turned for the moment. When the Battle of Cambrai began on November 20, the British had four times as many aircraft on the front as the Germans and ten times as many fighters.

The Germans had temporarily lost control of the air, and their soldiers were retreating on the ground. But these reverses had not been serious enough to cause alarm. On November 20 the British lost 35 percent of the low-flying planes that went out to cooperate with the ground troops, and two days later nineteen aircraft went out on strafing missions and only eleven returned.

By the end of the month the Germans had stopped the British advance and managed to push it back a mile and a half beyond the starting point. This success was due, in part, to thirty ground-strafing planes that had been held in reserve. These machines, with their specially trained crews, operated so effectively that they inflicted heavy casualties on the British and, according to the official historian, "demoralized our troops."

At this point it was the Allies who were apprehensive, while the Germans again had visions of victory. The British and French had advanced slightly, but with great losses. The British lost 400,000 men at Ypres and another 45,000 at Cambrai. Meanwhile, the French had suffered so heavily for meaningless, small ground gains that some of the troops mutinied.

Several other events made the future seem brighter for the Germans. Russia had been knocked out of the war, meaning that German troops and supplies could be transferred to the Western Front. At the same time, the Allies had suffered disaster on the Italian Front. The line had been broken by the Austro-German attack at Caporetto, where 300,000 Italians were captured and another estimated 300,000 deserted. To prevent a complete German victory against the Italians, the British and French rushed thousands of ground soldiers from France to Italy, along with three squadrons of R.F.C. aircraft. On top of all this, the submarine campaign against the British was continuing to take an appalling toll of shipping.

Adding further problems was the fact that bombing raids against England had been intensified. Between September 24 and October 1 there was a raid every night except one. During just one of these attacks, 14,000 rounds of antiaircraft shells were fired at the attackers without bringing one of them down.

The Gothas had now been joined by Zeppelin Giants, which were the most remarkable airplanes produced by the Germans during the war. These huge machines had wing spans of up to 138 feet 6 inches and were powered by as many as six engines. The horizontal tail surfaces alone were equal to the wing spans of most single-seat fighters. They were able to carry up to 4,400 pounds of bombs. On some special missions they went out with the largest bombs developed during the war: 2,200-pounders.

The British had won the air, but home flight training had not kept pace with requirements for replacements. Their estimate for replacements had been based on an average of two and a half months in combat for a fighter pilot and four months for two-seaters. In fact, the combat life of pilots was far shorter than had been anticipated.

British losses in flying personnel increased from 19.2 percent per month at the Battle of the Somme to 50 percent per month during the Battle of Arras. At the same time, German losses of flight crews was an average of only 12.5 percent per month. This smaller average for the Germans was due to better training, and also because they generally preferred to fight near the lines or over their own territory. Thus, when a German plane was shot down the pilot often escaped with minor injuries and could fly again. By contrast, when an Allied plane went down behind enemy lines, even from engine failure, the pilot as well as the plane was lost.

"I am rather worried about some of the pilots that have been sent out here lately," Major Rothesay Wortley wrote from France on December 30, 1917. "To start with they can't *fly* . . . at least not well enough to be allowed to cross the lines." The average R.F.C. flight student was then receiving only forty-eight and a half hours of flying time, but some were sent to France with as little as twenty-five hours total flying time!

Major Wortley continued, "To send them out to Squadrons in the field in a state of unfittedness to perform their proper share of the work in the Squadron is not only unfair to the 'young entry' themselves, but also unfair to the Flight Commanders under whose orders they come, and who are responsible for their efficiency. It is also unfair on their fellow Flying Officers who have to bear the burden of the extra work due to their having to take the places in the patrols which the former are yet unqualified to fill."

And so, at the end of 1917 the British and French were exhausted. They had fought their hardest in the air and on the land and sea, and yet the end was nowhere in sight. They were preparing to go on the defensive, hoping that the United States would arrive in time, and in sufficient force, to beat back the enemy. They were anticipating that 1918 would be a holding action, and that victory would come the following year.

The German plans were far different. They were preparing for an all-out offensive with their new manpower strength from the Russian Front. And they were hoping to be able to end the war early in 1918, before the massive fresh American armies could arrive and tip the scales against them.

Tension in the Air

Chapter Eleven

WHEN THE UNITED STATES declared war on Germany on April 6, 1917, the country's military air force was in pathetic condition. While thousands of pilots were being trained in Europe and modern fighting aircraft were rapidly being rolled off production lines, the United States had nothing but antiquated equipment.

Total U.S. aerial strength at that time consisted of sixty-five officers in the Aviation Section of the Signal Corps, only thirty-five of whom were pilots, plus 1,087 enlisted men. The U.S. Navy had thirty-eight pilots and 163 enlisted men with aviation ratings, plus five officers and thirty men of the Marine Corps. During the entire period from the invention of the airplane through almost three years of the war raging in Europe, the United States military had purchased only 142 airplanes, the majority of which had been pushers, and not one of them mounted a gun. The aviation industry in the country that had given birth to the flying machine was geared to a production of twelve to fifteen planes a year.

"We could boast fifty-five training planes," General John Pershing wrote, "all valueless for service at the front. Of these fifty-five planes, the National Advisory Committee for Aeronautics advised that fifty-one were obsolete and the other four obsolescent. We could not have put a single squadron in the field, although it was estimated later that we should eventually need at least 300 squadrons, each to be composed on the average of some twenty-four officers, 180 men, and eighteen airplanes, besides a large reservoir of planes for replacements."

Against this background, Premier Alexandre Ribot of France made a request on May 23 that was staggering. He wanted America to reinforce Allied airpower on the Western Front by providing 5,000 pilots, 50,000 ground personnel, and 4,500 combat airplanes plus replacements by early 1918. This actually meant production of approximately 12,000 service planes as well as 9,900 training aircraft, which would require 43,800 engines. These totals, large as they were, were shortly increased to 22,625 airplanes, plus 80 percent spares. The request was approved on June 27, and a month later Congress appropriated $640,000,000—at that date the largest sum ever appropriated for a single purpose—to build these airplanes and engines as soon as possible.

For the first time, the Aviation Section had been given serious attention. According to plans hastily drawn up, military aviation would be expanded to 345 combat squadrons, forty-five construction companies, eighty-one supply squadrons, eleven repair squadrons, and twenty-six balloon companies. Of this number, 263 squadrons were intended for use in Europe by June 1918.

The plans were grandiose, but there had not been enough military aviation experience. The first U.S. tactical aviation unit, the First Aero Squadron, had been organized in 1913 in San Diego, California, but its experience had been sad. On March 15, 1916, the squadron began operations at Columbus, New Mexico, as part of the expedition across the Mexican border against Pancho Villa. Its equipment consisted of eight airplanes, all of which were in poor condition.

On its initial mission, the eight-plane squadron was ordered to Casas Grandes, Mexico. One plane turned back to Columbus with a defective engine, three more became lost and were forced to land, and the other four made emergency landings due to darkness.

The squadron remained on the border for a month, carrying mail and dispatches, and scouting. On April 22 it returned to Columbus, its first war service finished. Six of the eight planes had been abandoned or destroyed, and the remaining two were condemned as unfit for further service.

In an effort to improve the production capacity of American airplane factories, the Aircraft Production Board was established just a month after Congress declared war. The existing aeronautical industry did not have the facilities to meet the task with which it was faced. However, the automobile industry, with its mass-production methods, claimed it would be able to build 100,000 airplanes within two years. The members of the Aircraft Production Board believed the automobile manufacturers, even though these companies knew virtually nothing about aviation. The mistake was costly, almost disastrous.

While Congressmen in Washington made statements about how the United States would "darken the skies" with airplanes, the industry was at a standstill. It had no plans for modern aircraft; it had no experience in mass production; it did not have sufficient supplies of spruce for construction or linen for covering wings and fuselages; and it had no factories as such. America had pledged itself to support its allies, but the problems were enormous.

One of the first large orders was placed with the Curtiss Company for production of its JN-4, which had actually been designed by B. Douglas Thomas of the British Sopwith Company. The JN-4, more familiarly known as the Jenny, was adopted as the primary pilot-training plane along with the Standard SJ.

Since the United States had no acceptable military combat aircraft of its own design, the Bolling Commission selected the British D.H.4 as one of the foreign types for home production. The decision was not wise, for the D.H.4, though outstanding for its day, was already approaching obsolescence. But the decision was made and tooling was started. At the same time,

Major H.A. Dargue and his Curtiss JN Jenny were forced down near Chihuahua City during the American expedition into Mexico. The U.S. Aviation Section's operation was a failure. *U.S. Air Force*

there were no aircraft engines in the United States capable of powering the D.H.4.

Two noted motorcar engineers, who had also produced aircraft power plants, were given the task of designing a suitable engine. These men, Jesse Vincent and J.G. Hall, went into seclusion in a hotel room and remained there for five days. Working on alternate twenty-four-hour shifts, they produced plans for a V-8 engine with light steel cylinders that would deliver up to 300 horsepower. Twenty-eight days after they started on their plans, the first engines were ready for testing.

The Liberty, as the engine was called, was the best aircraft engine that had been developed in the United States. However, it had several drawbacks. It had been designed to operate with castor oil for lubrication, and castor oil could not be found anywhere in the quantities that would be required. This led to the importation of castor beans from India, and more than 100,000 acres were planted. After the first crop, scientists developed a better lubricating oil, and the farmers were left with huge quantities of castor beans and no market for them.

Production was started on the Liberty engines, only to be halted almost immediately. Events were changing so quickly over the fighting fronts that the 300-horsepower American engine was already outmoded. The engineers went back to their drawing boards, redesigning their engine for twelve cylinders, boosting the output to 400 horsepower.

A number of serious mistakes were made as industry tried to build not just airplanes but all the things that had to go into them. One of the greatest errors was the optimism of the automobile makers, who thought they could turn out airplanes in volume. Such estimates, made publicly, encouraged the public to expect a production miracle that did not come off.

In an ill-advised effort to make things look better than they actually were, in June 1917 General George O. Squier, Chief of the Aviation Section, issued a statement that read in part, "We are sending myriads of airplanes over the German lines to teach Germany that we have come to win." Not one American-

built airplane had been sent to France. The first U.S. built
D.H.4 was not even flown until October 29, 1917.

Several other factors contributed to the failure of the United
States to put a great air force into the field. After production
was finally started and the first models were delivered to the
military for testing, requested design changes held up production still longer. Manufacturing problems caused by these alterations were made more difficult by the lack of qualified
engineers.

But while the word at home was confusion, a number of
Americans had already entered the war. One of the first of
those to wear wings was Norman Prince of Prides Crossing,
Massachusetts. At the outbreak of war, Prince offered his services to France as a volunteer aviator. He was accepted, and
early in March of the following year, he began flight training
at the Military Aviation School at Pau.

Norman Prince wanted to do more than just fly for France.
He conceived the idea of forming an aviation squadron composed exclusively of Americans. However, the French Government turned him down, insisting that they already had more
aviators than they could use. Even with this, Prince continued
his efforts. Finally, with the assistance of several influential
Americans, including Dr. Edmund Gros, who had lived in Paris
for many years, a unique law was passed which allowed Americans with previous flying experience to be accepted into a
special unit.

Elliot Cowdin, one of the original members of the *Escadrille
Américaine,* which was later changed to *Escadrille Lafayette
N.124,* wrote about the formation of the group:

Early in May 1916, we were all mobilized at the Alsatian front as
the Lafayette Squadron, with French officers, Captain [Georges]
Thénault and Lieutenant de Laage, in command. The original
members, besides those officers, were Norman Prince, William
Thaw, Victor Chapman, and Kiffin Rockwell, of the Foreign
Legion; James McConnell, who had already done good work in
the American Ambulance before joining the French Aviation; Bert

Hall, and myself. We remained but a short time in Alsace and were then transferred to the Verdun sector.

Several other Americans joined the *escadrille* after it arrived at the fighting front. Among these was Raoul Lufbery, who had joined the Foreign Legion in 1914, first as an airplane mechanic and then as a pilot in *Escadrille de Bombardment VB.106.*

On May 18, 1916, in its fourth day of operation at the front, Kiffin Rockwell scored the group's first victory. That same day Clyde Balsley, shot down and seriously wounded, was the first casualty. The following month Victor Chapman became the first American pilot to die in the war, when the wings of his Nieuport fighter collapsed during combat with two German planes. Kiffin Rockwell was the next to die. Then, on October 15, Norman Prince was killed when his plane struck high-tension wires during a landing approach. He had scored five official victories.

While the men of the *Lafayette Escadrille* were trained by the French Government, this was done at the expense of other Americans living in France. Pay for these gallant flyers was five cents a day, but they were also offered a bonus of $250 plus two days' leave in Paris for every enemy aircraft shot down.

By the time the United States entered the war, four of the *escadrille's* original seven members, plus eleven replacements, had been killed. At the end of 1917, a total of 267 Americans had joined the Lafayette Flying Corps (of which the *Lafayette Escadrille* was a part). Twenty-five of these died in action, others were killed in flying accidents, and several more were wounded or taken prisoner. By the time the Lafayette Flying Corps was transferred to American command in 1918, fifty-one of its members had been killed in combat, another eleven were dead from crashes or illness, nineteen had been wounded, and fifteen captured. Against these losses, the group claimed 199 German airplanes shot down. The most outstanding of these American pilots in terms of victories was Lufbery, who had scored seventeen officially confirmed.

Morane-Saulnier MS-12 Roleurs were used to teach American pilot trainees how to taxi. Called "grass cutters," the Roleurs did not have enough power to leave the ground.   *U.S. Air Force*

The first American aviation unit to reach France was the original First Aero Squadron. However, it arrived without guns or planes and with no experience in combat flying and little knowledge of modern tactics. The squadron arrived on September 3, 1917, with Major Ralph Royce in command, and immediately went into training at French flying schools.

Meanwhile, Germany was gathering its resources for an offensive unmatched by anything thus far in the war. They were still transporting troops and supplies from the Russian Front to the main conflict in France. At the same time, they had decided to make a supreme effort with their air force, supplying it with large numbers of the most modern airplanes available. To this end, a competition for single-seat biplane fighters was announced, to be held in January 1918. Actual combat pilots were to test these machines and make their own selections. The Johannisthal airdrome near Berlin was selected as the site for the competitions.

Every manufacturer quickly went to the drawing boards to design planes based on three years of combat experience. Within six weeks the Pfalz Flugzeugwerke had its D-3A ready. Other competitors were Albatros, Aviatik, Roland, Rumpler, Kondor, Schutte-Lanz, and Siemens-Schuckert. Another entry was a Fokker, then identified as the V-11.

The V-11 had been designed by Fokker and Reinhold Platz, and it was an angular little biplane with thick wings. There was very little attempt at streamlining. Whereas the Albatros D-3 and other planes had been designed with great care to prevent as much drag from the slipstream as possible, the Fokker had a square fuselage. Simplicity was the keynote of the plane. Fokker had wanted a machine that would be easy to build and easy to fly. At the same time, it was one of the strongest airplanes ever made. The upper wing was straight and continuous, without a separate center section, and the spars of the lower wing extended through the fuselage; this, in effect, meant that the lower wing was also a single-unit construction.

When the first experimental model of the new machine was

ready, Tony Fokker took it up himself for testing. He flew it for several hours, going through every conceivable maneuver. When Fokker landed, he was both pleased and concerned. He felt that it was the most maneuverable airplane he had ever flown and was capable of doing things that even he had not expected. At the same time, it had a tendency to spin, and its responsiveness to controls was actually too quick for the average pilot. In the hands of an experienced man, the fighter was beautiful to fly; but for an inexperienced fledgling, it was too dangerous.

Two days before the competition was scheduled to be held, Fokker decided that the only way to correct the problem would be to lengthen the fuselage. That night and the next day he and three of his men worked on the machine, welding in an extra length of fuselage and increasing the size of the vertical fin. After these alterations had been made, Fokker took the plane up again, and he was delighted with the results. It retained the climbing ability and other performance characteristics of the original version, but was no longer dangerous to fly. He landed with confidence that his entry would win the competition.

Fokker's plane was to become the famous D-7, which was the best fighter built in quantity by the Germans during the war and possibly the best built by any of the warring nations. During the tests at Johannisthal, it literally forced all of the competing machines out of the sky. The Albatros, Rumpler, and Pfalz were faster than the Fokker, but they could not climb as well or maneuver as well. All in all, it was a fighting man's airplane.

It has been a popular supposition for many years that the Fokker D-7 was a demon for speed, that it could turn quickly with the throttle cracked wide, and that it could dive away from a combat faster than any of its opponents. These suppositions were all incorrect.

The Fokker D-7 was not especially fast; it had a maximum speed of only 116.5 miles per hour at 3,280 feet, while at 9,840

While the Americans were still trying to get into the air war, Anthony Fokker in Germany came up with his D-7, which was possibly the best fighter used by either side.   *U.S. Air Force*

feet its speed dropped to 110. By comparison, the Spad S-13 could do 128 miles per hour at 9,800 feet and the Sopwith Camel was able to achieve a speed of 124 at 6,500 feet.

The Fokker's unique ability was displayed not at high speed, but at speeds just above the stalling point, and this was due to the high-lift thick wings. While other aircraft were mushy on the controls at low speeds or high altitudes, the Fokker still retained its extraordinary maneuverability. According to pilots who flew it in combat or who fought against it, the Fokker could literally hang on its propeller at speeds of about 35 miles per hour and continue to respond to the controls. This gave the plane its reputation for making good pilots out of fair ones and experts out of good pilots.

After the trials had been completed, Anthony Fokker was awarded a contract for 400 machines of the D-7 type, with instructions to rush them into production without delay. The plane was also ordered into production by Albatros at both of its plants. General von Hoeppner's program called for standardization of equipment, and the Fokker was to be Germany's first-line fighter. Aircraft were also ordered from several of the other companies competing in this first of the D-type trials. These went into production to provide a continuing flow of replacements and to backstop Fokker in the event of unexpected delays.

One of the new fighters ordered in limited numbers was the Roland D-6B, which has been described as "the most elegant of all German single-seat fighters." A captured Roland was tested by the United States after the war had ended, and the test pilot, Lieutenant Louis Moriarty, wrote in his report, "The flying qualities of this airplane are very similar to those of the Fokker D-7. Its controls have about the same degree of effectiveness but operate more easily. Its maneuverability is well above that of the average single-seater."

General von Hoeppner's plans for his air force in connection with the coming offensive were grand in conception. In 1915 the Germans produced 4,532 aircraft, 3,986 of which were trainers and observation-bombers. In 1916 the figure was almost doubled to 8,179. In 1917 production reached a total of 19,746, with the emphasis still on two-seaters. For the new year of 1918, the goal was 2,000 airplanes and 2,500 aircraft engines per month.

Something else was also happening directly behind the front lines. Whereas previously there had been an airdrome spotted here and there, the Germans now started building hangars and clearing fields at regular intervals. The Allies did not understand the reason for this new construction, since most of the fields were empty of aircraft, but they were soon to find out. An ingenious plan had been formulated to give the German Air Force greater mobility. Instead of being restricted to certain operational areas because of the locations of their flying fields, they would now be able to shift from field to field as required. These new airfields gave them the ability to achieve local force and superiority for short periods of time.

Jagdgeschwader 1 had been formed under Baron Manfred von Richthofen on June 26, 1917, as an experiment. By the end of the year the experiment had proved itself, and other such hunting groups were created, each of them under the command of an outstanding leader.

This was a time of tension for the British and French. It was assumed that the enemy was bringing up new troops in a regular stream, but aerial reconnaissance failed to locate them. From December 1, 1917, until February 15, 1918, the French and British sent aircraft out almost constantly in an effort to learn what was happening behind the lines. During this period the French alone flew 22,518 reconnaissance missions, including 1,399 photographic flights. However, the weather was too poor for accurate spotting, and no real news was brought back. It later became known that the Germans had been moving troops by night in an effort to avoid detection, and then dispersing them in towns and villages during daylight hours.

The Allies knew something was being planned, but they weren't sure what. The French felt that the drive would be against Paris, and the British thought it would be against the Channel ports to cut the supply lines. Because of this indecision, large reinforcements and supply depots were concentrated behind each of the fronts, to be thrown into battle if and when necessary.

During these days of anxious waiting for the storm to break, the task of the fighting squadrons was lighter than it had been previously. The R.F.C. and the French went on the defensive, and the Germans conserved their strength for the big push. The major activity was by the observation planes and bombers. During one single night No. 101 Squadron of the R.F.C. was sent to strike at eight airdromes, five railway stations, and eight villages where it was assumed that German infantrymen were billeted.

Day after day the observation planes and kite balloons spotted for the heavy artillery, which was attempting to cause as much destruction as possible to weaken the attack. The big guns were directed at artillery dumps and railroad lines and also poured fire at roads and even paths in an effort to make movement of supplies more difficult.

Moving troops by night to avoid detection proved so successful for the Germans that they also started to bring up supplies under the cover of darkness. At first the Allies were puzzled by the large number of lights that began showing in rear areas after the sun went down. Aerial reconnaissance finally located a number of strange white objects. Long-range artillery was zeroed in on these boxes, and several of them exploded, showing that they were boxes of ammunition. After that other artillery pieces were ranged on the area, and more than 100 explosions were counted.

In this period the largest air battles resulted from attacks on German aviation facilities. One very large combat took place when approximately fifty German fighters climbed up to drive off bombers over Busigny. In this engagement nine British planes fell against four German losses.

While the fighting powers were getting ready for the land battle, the United States was still attempting to get into the war in force. On February 20, in an obvious effort to help bolster the morale of the American people, Secretary of War Newton Baker announced that the first U.S.-built aircraft were en route to France, "nearly five months ahead of schedule."

"In making this announcement," newspapers reported, "Secretary Baker said that the first shipment, although in itself not large, 'marks the final overcoming of many difficulties in building up this new and intricate industry.'"

Secretary Baker explained that after three years of war the total number of aircraft able to take to the air at any one time on either side of the Western Front had not been more than 2,500. Mr. Baker went on to say that forty-six men were required on the ground for every plane in the air, "making a total of 115,000 men needed for the present maximum of 2,500 planes."

But what the Secretary did not explain was that this first token shipment of D.H.4's would not reach France until May. The British and French had been counting heavily upon the United States to supply them with airplanes in time to meet the German spring offensive. However, it actually became necessary for the Americans to purchase aircraft from their European allies. By the time the Armistice was signed, the United States had received 4,881 airplanes from the French, 258 from the British, and nineteen from the Italians.

At the time of Secretary Baker's announcement, a New York banker and mining executive named William Potter had just taken over as Chief of the Equipment Division. Mr. Potter has been described as a "keen, tough, sensible manager," and one of his first actions was to call Glenn Martin to Washington and request that he go ahead with the MB-1 bomber, which had previously been turned down in favor of building the D.H.4. Mr. Potter also arranged for the Chance Vought Company to build a new training plane, Thomas-Morse to design a single-seat fighter, and Loening to produce a two-seat fighter. These were the first truly modern aircraft ever ordered for the Aviation Section, and when they finally appeared they were surprisingly successful.

"The Martin MB-1 bomber was not only ahead of any foreign war bomber," Grover Loening wrote, "but continued for years afterward to lead in its class. The Loening two-seat fighter —a new design of strut-braced monoplane—was lighter, faster, climbed higher, and outflew the Bristol Fighter then in use at the front. The Vought and the Thomas-Morse also were far superior to their European rivals."

A short time later General Squier was relieved of his post as head of the Aviation Section of the Signal Corps and all responsibility for military aviation was passed over to the Army, with General William Kenly in command. These were important changes and were to prove valuable in the future. However, the United States aviation establishment was still in a bad way early in 1918.

The first Americans even to get a look at the trenches from the cockpits of airplanes were those of the 94th Aero Squadron. The commanding officer of the group was Raoul Lufbery, and he selected Edward Rickenbacker and Douglas Campbell to accompany him on the flight. The date was March 6, and the aircraft they flew were unarmed French Nieuports.

"I had joined the Hat-in-the-Ring Squadron just two days before at Villeneuve," Rickenbacker wrote. "We were then some twenty miles behind the lines and were well installed on an old aerodrome that had been used previously by several French Aero Squadrons. This expedition was to be the first essay over the lines by a made-in-America Squadron."

The following morning at eight o'clock the three-ship formation took off. Before climbing into their cockpits, however, Lufbery warned Rickenbacker and Campbell to stay close to him, promising that he would watch out for them. They went up to 15,000 feet and headed toward the lines. Rickenbacker wrote:

We had been sailing along at this dizzy height for some thirty minutes between Reims and the Argonne Woods when it occurred to me to look below at the landscape. And such a spectacle spread itself out before my eyes when I at last did look over the side of my little office!

The trenches in this sector were quite old and had remained in practically the same position for three years of warfare. To my inexperienced view there appeared to be nothing below me but old battered trenches, trench works, and billions of shell holes which had dug up the whole surface of the earth for four or five miles on either side of me. Not a tree, not a fence, no sign of any familiar occupation of mankind, nothing but a chaos of ruin and desolation. The awfulness of the thing was truly appalling.

After two hours Lufbery led his two fledglings back to their field, where he asked if they had seen any other airplanes in the sky. Both Campbell and Rickenbacker agreed that they had been entirely alone, with no other aircraft in sight.

"Just what I expected," Lufbery replied. "They're all the same." After a pause he went on, "One formation of five Spads crossed under us before we passed the lines and another flight of five Spads went by about fifteen minutes later and you didn't see them, although neither one of them was more than 500 yards away. It was just as well they were not Boches!

"Then there were four German Albatros two miles ahead of us when we turned back," Lufbery continued, "and there was another enemy two-seater nearer us than that, at about 5,000 feet above the lines."

Major Lufbery then walked over to Rickenbacker's plane and pointed out that the flight had not been as uneventful as the two new pilots may have thought. Shrapnel from antiaircraft had punched three holes in the Nieuport: one in the tail, another through the wing, and a third had torn through both wings not a foot from the cockpit.

"The boys told me afterwards that I stayed pale for a good thirty minutes," Rickenbacker admitted.

The Americans had arrived, but they were faced with many problems. Because of unbelievable mix-ups, some squadrons

In the beginning, American pilots had to be content with any aircraft they could get. One type supplied to them was the old Bréguet 14, which was badly outmoded. *U.S. Air Force*

were receiving planes but no guns while others were being supplied with guns but no planes.

"What have we done in our year of war?" Lieutenant Raymond Clyde Taylor wrote to his parents in Billerica, Massachusetts. "I hope to get to the front by the time this letter reaches you, but there seem to be so many side-tracks and the French are quite able to fly their own planes and the British are too darned good flyers to take any chances on greenhorns. Our only hope is to borrow an old bus from somewhere. It's a shame that many of us have been in training for over a year and we haven't had a look at the Boches yet. We want guns, bullets, and planes and we want them badly."

Lieutenant Taylor finally got his "old bus," a French Bréguet two-seater. On his last flight, six planes in his squadron started out on a mission, two of them returning because of engine trouble. Of the four remaining, three were shot down in flames. The only surviving Bréguet was a newer model that had been equipped with an armored fuel tank.

While the Americans were forced to be content with any aircraft they could get, the British had developed a new machine, which was later called "the best all-round Allied fighter of the war." This was the Sopwith Snipe.

The Snipe did not achieve the high victories of the Camel or S.E.5, but this was because the plane arrived at the front too late to display its real capabilities. By the time of the Armistice, only three squadrons had been supplied with the machines. One of these, No. 43 Squadron, achieved thirty-six victories in only four days with their new equipment. A Snipe was also flown by Major William Barker in his epic battle against an entire German *jagdschwader* on October 27, 1918.

The Snipe was planned as a replacement for the Camel. It was one of the first fighting machines to be designed around an engine—the new 230-horsepower Bentley. The basic design was originated in 1917, and after five experimental models had been built for tests, 1,900 examples were ordered from six contractors.

While the Snipe was not particularly fast, it had excellent climbing and handling characteristics, making it a worthy foe for the Fokker D-7. Its maximum speed was 121 miles per hour at 10,000 feet and its service ceiling 20,000 feet.

This new plane was evidence that the British could see no end to the war. The Americans had not yet contributed substantially to the conflict, and the enemy was still powerful. Anything could happen, and they wanted to be ready.

New Wings Arrive

Chapter Twelve

DESPITE ITS CAREFUL PREPARATIONS, the German Air Force was not up to anticipated strength by March 1, 1918. The new Fokker D-7's had not yet started to arrive from the factories and there had been unexpected delays in production of other types. However, for the first time they were able to achieve a numerical superiority of front-line machines over the British. The R.F.C. had a total of 579 airplanes, including 261 fighters, in operational squadrons; against this force, the Germans had 730 machines in battle squadrons, including 326 single-seat fighters.

On the evening of March 20 a thick fog spread over the entire area between Arras and St. Quentin. This could not have been better for the Germans, since the troops under General Hans von Bülow had received orders to strike the following morning. During the night the front became strangely quiet as the German artillery stopped its pounding. This was the calm before the storm. At 4:45 in the morning the shells thundered down in a hail, pulverizing the ground as far as twenty miles behind the front-line trenches. Following this intense barrage, the infantry moved forward across the pitted ground of No Man's Land. The fog was so thick that many British soldiers in forward machine-gun positions did not even know the attack had started until the Germans were behind them.

While the Germans were smashing at their enemies south of Arras, another wave broke at the combined British and French forces near St. Quentin. Until this time the Allies had felt the St. Quentin area was so well fortified that it was virtually impregnable.

As the fog began to lift later in the morning of March 21, German planes came over in droves, flying low and adding more confusion to the Allies with ground-strafing. Even the fighters, flying only slightly higher than the army cooperation two-seaters, were called upon for ground-attack work.

Only one squadron of British R.E.8's was able to report success on reconnaissance missions. They spotted artillery emplacements, massed groups of enemy troops, and infantrymen moving forward. But while this intelligence was sent back, there was little answering artillery fire. Most of the British big guns were being moved to the rear or had been put out of action by German artillery.

Meanwhile, an order came for the D.H.4 squadrons to attack enemy railroad lines, bridges, and roads. These raids were practically useless, since they were made from an altitude of 15,000 feet with bombs weighing only twenty-five pounds. The bombers were kept at high altitude because of a directive issued the previous autumn in an effort to conserve the then-valuable D.H.4's; months later, when the machines were plentiful, the order still had not been rescinded! Air Commodore J.A. Chamier wrote, "To bomb vital targets with twenty-five-pound bombs from 15,000 feet was a sheer waste of attacking power and betrays a very poor appreciation of the situation by the higher air command."

During the first two days of the battle each side lost about thirty planes. The fog continued through the third day of the engagement, though lifting slightly. With this relief in flying conditions the war in the air became intensified and each side lost approximately forty planes.

On Sunday, March 24, the weather turned still better. On that day forty-two German planes were destroyed while the R.F.C. lost seventy-five from all causes, including eight that were set afire and abandoned in the face of the enemy advance.

The outstanding British fighter pilot of that day was Captain George McElroy. While McElroy had joined No. 40 Squadron in August 1917, he did not score his first victory until December 28. Then his successes came rapidly, surprising no one more than himself, for he did not think he was a particularly good pilot. What he may have lacked in flying ability, he made up in gunnery. Many of his victories were achieved at long range, and an analysis of twenty of his combats revealed that he averaged only 130 rounds of ammunition per combat.

During January 1918 McElroy shot down a plane a day for eight days; in this same period he also destroyed three balloons. His work was so outstanding that he was transferred from No. 40 Squadron and made a flight leader of No. 24 Squadron. To this day the manner of McElroy's death has never been established. While his bullet-riddled S.E.5a was found where it crashed on July 31, 1918, the pilot was not in the cockpit or any place in the vicinity.

George McElroy was undoubtedly one of the deadliest fighter pilots of the war. His biggest day was on March 24, 1918. On that single day, he claimed no less than six German two-seaters!

While there were numerous cases of daring among the opposing airmen, the German infantrymen were carrying the battle more conclusively than any engagement in the war since the opening rounds in 1914. Their attack was overpowering, forcing the British back so rapidly that their retreat was close to a rout. Adding further to their difficulties, the British were hit heavily in the rear areas. In one notable night mission against Amiens and Longueau, an ammunition convoy of forty-one trucks was completely destroyed.

March 24 brought no let-up for the Allies, and their ground forces were pushed back still more. All available British aircraft were again ordered to work in cooperation with the ground forces. "Very low flying is essential," read the order from Major General W. G. Salmond. "All risks to be taken." The men of the R.F.C. responded with their best efforts, and thirty-seven squadrons were thrown into the effort. All aircraft, including fighters, went out loaded to capacity with bombs. One of these was shot down by Baron von Richthofen for his sixty-eighth victory, and the bombs exploded after the plane crashed in flames near Bapaume.

As example of the amount of support given their retreating troops, that one day the British airmen dropped 117 230-pound bombs and 1,300 twenty-five-pounders and also poured almost 250,000 rounds of ammunition into the ranks of the advancing enemy. This slowed the attack but did not halt it. The Germans were suffering heavy losses and their troops were tired, but they had not yet been hurt enough to be forced to stop to regroup. This battle had to succeed if victory was to be won, and the Germans wanted an end to the war as much as anyone. They had been bled white. Their resources in men and machines were constantly dwindling.

That single month of March was the bloodiest of the air war to date. The Germans shot down 340 Allied planes, and scores of others were lost through crashes or deliberately destroyed by the retreating R.F.C. German losses were also considerable. The British alone demolished 362 enemy aircraft and damaged another 205. Added to this, France accounted for 107 German airplanes destroyed and fifty-two damaged. This total of 469 machines lost in combat weakened the German front-line force considerably, and they were forced to bring up large numbers of reserves.

Fortunately for their cause, the Germans had more than enough planes available in the depots. In the Arras area they increased their force to 822 aircraft against 645 for the R.F.C. However, the British maintained a superiority of two to one to the north of Arras, while to the south the French had five to one.

On April 1, while it was suffering large losses, the Royal Flying Corps became an independent command on an equal footing with the army and navy. The future of the British air arm had never appeared more uncertain, but on that date its name was changed to the Royal Air Force.

With their advance going well but not decisively, the Germans now turned their attention to the front north of Arras— and again heavy fog clouds moved in. The R.A.F. bases were in danger of being overrun and several of them were ordered evacuated. However, the ceiling was too low for flying in some cases, and at least one squadron, No. 208, set fire to its eighteen Sopwith Camels before retreating.

The battle wore on, with the British taking the brunt of the offensive directed against it. On April 12 Field Marshal Sir Douglas Haig issued his famous order, "With our backs to the wall, and believing in the justice of our cause, each one of us must fight on to the end."

At this point, the German advance almost abruptly slowed to a crawl. This was due to a number of things. The British had called up French reserves, the Germans had lost too many men and those still in combat were exhausted from the incessant fighting, and the advance had been so rapid that supplies could not be brought up quickly enough. The Germans had swept some forty miles farther into Allied territory and were almost at the gates of Paris; then they were forced to stop, bloody and battered and short of the victory they had anticipated.

The Germans were closer to victory than they knew. Charles Veil, an American who had preferred to remain with the French rather than transfer to an American unit, explained this in his outspoken autobiography, *Adventure's a Wench:*

Between Montdidier and Amiens the Fifth English Army had left the trenches. This retreat has been soft-pedaled, but it's a fact. It was said that the officers would not speak to the non-coms, and the non-coms would not speak to the Tommies so the Tommies up and walked out. We could see the retreat from the air and couldn't believe our eyes when we saw for the first and only time during

The French had depended upon the Americans to supply them with airplanes. Instead, the U.S. Air Service was forced to buy planes from the French. This is a Nieuport 27 in American service.

U.S. Air Force

A captured Rumpler C-4. The plane had good performance at high altitudes, and few Allied fighters could catch it above 15,000 feet. This machine was forced down by the French.   *U.S. Air Force*

this man's war cavalry charging toward the front—Canadian troopers striving desperately to block the gap. The retreat became a rout, leaving nothing in the trenches except a few platoons of *poilus*. The Germans could easily have broken through there, straight to Paris by the shortest route. Where was the famed German Secret Service? Why didn't the German headquarters know of the situation? Why didn't the German observation planes get over our trenches and find them empty?

"Our flyers could answer only the latter question," Veil continued. "No German plane crossed that line." Not because they did not try, but because Veil and his comrades kept them out.

On the morning of April 14, while the great battle still raged on the ground, an historic event took place. This was the day the first American squadron finally went into action, and the day the first American aerial victories were scored.

The previous evening the orders had come through to the 94th Pursuit Squadron and had been posted on the Operations Board. They stated simply that Captain David Peterson and Lieutenants Reed Chambers and Edward Rickenbacker would start a patrol of the lines the following morning at six o'clock. Their flight altitude was to be 16,000 feet and the patrol was to extend from Pont-à-Mousson on the Moselle to St. Mihiel on the Meuse, a distance of eighteen miles. The order also stated that the patrol was to be of a duration of two hours, and that Lieutenants Douglas Campbell and Alan Winslow were to "stand by on the alert" from six o'clock until ten. This alert was provided in case of a sudden emergency, such as an enemy bombing raid or a call for assistance against German aircraft within the Allied lines.

This first patrol was anything but a success. Peterson soon dropped out and returned to the field. Rickenbacker assumed that the Captain had been forced back by engine trouble, but he later learned that Peterson had turned back because of heavy fog in the distance. But like the fledgling pilots they were, Rickenbacker and Chambers continued, oblivious to the dangerous flying weather.

"We picked up the valley of the Moselle River," Ricken-backer wrote later, "and proceeded blandly upon our way and would probably have kept on to the Rhine, but for a sudden bark under the tail of Chambers' machine which announced that we were discovered over German guns."

The two-plane patrol made four sweeps between Pont-à-Mousson and St. Mihiel and then turned toward home—only then discovering to their horror that the entire area was blanketed by fog. Flying cautiously by compass and altimeter, Rickenbacker made it back to Toul "by the sheerest good luck," but Chambers became lost and landed at a nearby airfield.

Within a few minutes a call came in that two German air-planes had been sighted over the neighboring village of Foug, and Campbell and Winslow, who had been standing by all morning, rushed to take off. Within three minutes Winslow brought down one of the Germans, while Campbell forced the second to crash—the infant squadron's first victories.

Neither of the German pilots was seriously injured. They explained that they had been sent out to intercept two Nieu-ports that had been flying between Pont-à-Mousson and St. Mihiel. They had followed Chambers and Rickenbacker, finally losing them in the fog. The Germans then tried to find their way back to their own airdrome near Metz, but they too became lost. At last they spotted the American flying field and came down low, thinking it might be their own. At this point, just 500 feet above the drome, they were attacked by Winslow and Campbell.

Fourteen days later, on April 29, Rickenbacker shot down his first enemy plane, an Albatros by the official records but a Pfalz according to Rickenbacker's own story.

Eight days before the American ace of aces started on his string of victories, the greatest of all German aces had his ended.

Manfred von Richthofen had grown weary of war. He had never been the same after being shot down the previous year. Although he was still a master pilot and a crack marksman, Richthofen's victories became fewer and farther apart during

The Nieuport 28 became the first standard American fighter. Lieutenants Douglas Campbell and Alan Winslow, flying Nieuports, were the first Americans to win victories. *U.S. Air Force*

the remainder of 1917. Then he was sent on an inspection tour of aviation facilities and did not return to the Western Front again until February 11. Beginning on March 12, he seemed more like himself again. That month he shot down eleven British planes—three of them on one day—and brought his total score to seventy-four. He was still going strong in April, with six more victories through the 20th of the month. His score was now an amazing eighty.

Richthofen's last victim was Lieutenant D.E. Lewis, in a Sopwith Camel. After he crashed in flames, though not injured, Lewis jumped out of his machine and tried to save Major Raymond Barker, who had also been shot down nearby and was still in the cockpit of his burning Camel.

Years later, writing about the fight, Lewis told about his miraculous escape. "The following articles [in his plane] were hit by Richthofen's bullets: the compass, which was directly in front of my face, my goggles where the elastic joined the frame of the glass—these went over the side—the elbow of my coat, and one bullet through the leg of my trousers."

Lewis admitted that the rest of his twelve-plane flight was saved from annihilation by the arrival of a squadron of S.E.5's. As the Germans beat a hasty retreat, Richthofen came down to within a hundred feet of the ground and waved a hand to his final vanquished foe.

On the morning of April 21, Richthofen prepared for battle as usual. On the way to his triplane he stopped to pat a dog, and a mechanic asked the ace if he could take a picture of him. Richthofen nodded his assent, thus breaking a superstition he had about being photographed before a patrol—a superstition which had begun when a photographer snapped a picture of Oswald Boelcke before his last flight.

That day, while pursuing his intended eighty-first victim, Richthofen was shot down and killed—and to this day arguments still flare over the identity of the victor. The Royal Air Force gave official credit to Captain A. Roy Brown, a Canadian pilot, while the official Australian history claims with equal authority and documentation that the German was brought down by ground fire from the 53rd Battery, Fifth Australian Division. It is interesting to note that in their combat reports following the action neither Captain Brown nor his wingman, Lieutenant Wilfred May, claimed that Brown had shot down Richthofen but merely a red triplane. After examining the various reports, one Australian wrote:

> With regard to Captain Brown's claim, I think that this can be ruled out, but there is one aspect I should like to mention, and that is the psychological point of view. The morale of the Royal Air Force needed a little bolstering up at that time, and any bending of the evidence to that end was thoroughly justified, and not to be grudged.

Three days later, after Richthofen had been buried with military honors, a Canadian pilot from No. 209 Squadron flew low over the German airdrome at Cappy. He threw over a metal cylinder that contained a photograph of the funeral party and a message, which read:

TO THE GERMAN FLYING CORPS
Rittmeister Baron Manfred von Richthofen was killed in aerial combat on April 21, 1918. He was buried with full military honours.
From the British Royal Air Force

The Allies were elated that their arch foe in the air had been defeated, and there was understandable gloom in Germany. They had lost a symbol of supposed invincibility who had buoyed up their morale when their armies were not doing well in the ground fighting. Even General Erich von Ludendorff, who had once expressed contempt for the military value of the airplane, commented that Richthofen alone had been worth as much to the German war effort as two divisions of infantry.

Within a month tragedy struck again, this time at the Allies. Jean Chaput, a French ace with sixteen victories, was shot out of the sky on May 18, and the following day Raoul Lufbery was brought down in flames.

Manfred von Richthofen was the highest-scoring fighter pilot of the war. He won 80 confirmed victories before he was shot down in his Fokker Dr.1 on April 21, 1918.

Lufbery's death was particularly tragic. He had carefully instructed the American pilots of his command in the art of flying and the business of killing, hoping that through his experience they might last longer in combat than most beginners. According to Rickenbacker, Lufbery told his young charges never to jump from their planes in case of fire. "I should always stay with the machine," he said. "If you jump you certainly haven't got a chance. On the other hand, there is always a good chance of side-slipping your airplane down in such a way that you fan the flames away from yourself and the wings."

That was one version. However, Bert Hall and Edwin Parsons insisted that Lufbery gave them another story: "If I get aflame, I'll jump. I'm not going to roast alive."

Around ten o'clock on the morning of May 19 a German plane identified as a two-seat Albatros—probably a J-1— appeared over St. Mihiel. An alert was telephoned to the drome of the 94th Pursuit Squadron, and Lieutenant Oscar Gude, the only pilot on the field ready to fight, climbed into his Nieuport and took off to intercept. This was Gude's first combat, and according to witnesses "he began firing at an impossible range and continued firing until his ammunition was exhausted."

Meanwhile, Lufbery had taken off to give chase. He had scored all of his victories on the German side of the lines and was anxious to bring one down on his own side.

"Within five minutes Luf was in range of the high-flying Hun and fired several short bursts as he closed in," according to Lieutenant LeRoy Prinz, one of the witnesses on the ground. "Then he veered away, apparently to clear a jammed gun. He zeroed in at point-blank range and fired several long bursts with absolutely no effect. He might as well have been firing feathers instead of bullets. We found out why later [the German was subsequently brought down by a French pilot]. The two-seater Albatros was armor plated.

"Suddenly," Prinz continued, "Raoul Lufbery's Nieuport 28 wobbled and tossed like a stick in a windstorm. A great ball of crimson flame fanned out from the cockpit. The agonized cry came from a hundred throats simultaneously, 'He's on fire!' "

Lufbery jumped from his flaming plane, in clear view of the assembled members of his squadron only six miles away. His body plummeted into the garden of a house just north of Nancy, where it was impaled on a picket fence. He was practically uninjured by enemy bullets. He had been hit only in the right thumb; the same bullet then plunged into the fuel tank, setting it on fire.

In May the Germans started receiving the new Fokker D-7's at the front—enough to equip several *jastas*—and the pilots soon discovered that these machines gave them a good margin of superiority. In April they had shot down 217 Allied planes, and in May the score zoomed to 413. It was to continue mounting month after month until the end of the war. According to official German records, from May through to the end of September their airmen brought down 2,737 enemy airplanes, which was only sixty-three less than the combined total of the entire years of 1916 and 1917. The German record for the first nine months of 1918, including balloons, amounted to 3,982, and this was 835 higher than the entire period from 1914 through to the end of 1917! No detailed German victory reports were issued for the last six weeks of the war.

The British had been hit badly. March and April cost them more than 1,000 airplanes out of the total they had in all front-line squadrons when the Germans launched their great offensive. This high rate of loss continued to accelerate in May. The hasty retreat had also cost the British 173 hangars, 1,738 bombs, and some 26,000 gallons of gasoline. The R.A.F. called these ground losses "surprisingly low," but the gasoline alone was a boon to the Germans, who had begun to run short on airplane fuel.

On March 31, Douglas Campbell shot down his fifth German airplane, a two-seat Rumpler, and became the first official American ace. That same day American infantrymen received their first taste of what war was really like. A small offensive was made northwest of Seicheprey, which was approximately midway between St. Mihiel and Pont-à-Mousson. The Doughboys surged out of their trenches behind an artillery barrage of some 20,000 rounds, and they were surprised by the lack of opposition. When they reached the German trenches they found only one enemy soldier, who was ill. The entire position had been deserted. Then, suddenly, they realized that they had fallen into a trap, for a hail of German shells started coming down, zeroed in on their own deserted trenches. The Americans were forced to retreat to their previous positions or face certain slaughter. Their casualties in this engagement, killed and wounded, amounted to about 300.

The following day, June 1, the United States activated the 27th and 147th Squadrons, which joined the 94th and 95th at the drome near Tours. Two days later a German plane came racing over and dropped a photograph of the American field, with a message on it: "Welcome 27th and 147th. Prepare to meet thy doom."

By this time the American fighter pilots had been credited with seventeen victories while suffering but four losses. They were soon to meet much stiffer opposition.

On June 28 the officers of all four American fighter squadrons operating from the field near Toul were called to Group Headquarters. The Group Commander was Major Atkinson, and the Operations Officer was Captain Philip Roosevelt, a cousin of President Theodore Roosevelt. Roosevelt gave the men some welcome news:

Gentlemen, we are about to be flattered and honored with some action. The German army, in desperation but with complete organization and consistency, is about to make a stupidly belated drive on Paris. Already some vital units of the civil government in Paris have been evacuated. The German attack will take place some time about the middle of July. The First American Pursuit Group has been chosen to join its gallant French and British comrades in the coming battle. We will be stationed halfway between the apex on the front lines and Paris, and we will do our job to the best of our ability.

The group's new home field was at Touquin, midway between Soissons and Reims, and only some eighteen miles behind the Château-Thierry salient. This was the deepest penetration the Germans had made toward Paris, which was only some thirty-seven miles away. The airdrome itself consisted of sixty acres of farmland.

Directly across the lines at Coincy, which was slightly north of Château-Thierry, was the old Richthofen *jasta*, now commanded by Wilhelm Reinhardt. There were also other hunting groups with seasoned leaders operating in this same area. Foremost among these were the units commanded by Bruno Loerzer, Hermann Goering, and Ernst Udet. These three were among the finest, most experienced pilots of the war. All three were also to survive the war, with a combined total of 125 confirmed victories.

There was no doubt that the Germans were still very powerful. In fact, if it had not been for the fresh American troops that were thrown into the Château-Thierry battle to bolster the French, it is questionable whether the line would have held. "I have never seen a more stunned group of people than the officers of the Third French Army headquarters," Colonel William Mitchell wrote, "and for that matter, the troops as well."

The Germans had paused, but everyone knew that another large blow was coming. Huge piles of ammunition were moved up, and General Ludendorff was massing troops to throw into the battle. Defeat was staring the Allies in the face.

General James Harbord wrote in his diary, "If the Germans do not bring off a very heavy offensive within the next few hours our French allies are going to explode, blow up, disintegrate, go off, flatten out, or undergo some other psychical and physical phenomenon."

On July 7, twenty British Sopwith Camels appeared over the

new American drome, then peeled off and landed. The following morning the entire R.A.F. Fifth Brigade landed at the field, with about 100 aircraft. These consisted of Camels, Bristol Fighters, and Handley Page bombers. The field was then so crowded with airplanes that the Americans moved three miles closer to the lines, to a place named Saiuts. This field was far smaller, but it was large enough for the Nieuports.

The Nieuport 28's handled well, but in many respects they were inferior to the Fokker D-7's facing them. "For the present, however," Rickenbacker wrote, "we had to take what was given to us. We felt that we were not fulfilling the expectations of the people back home, who had been told that we had 20,000 of the best aeroplanes in the world, and all made in America."

But one man, at least, was not content that the American fighting men should have to accept whatever ancient or outmoded aircraft they could get from the French. This was Colonel William Mitchell, who was one of the greatest and most outspoken advocates of airpower that any nation ever had. Mitchell had many violent arguments with his superiors over the quality and quantity of airplanes that had been supplied. He also objected to the way the existing equipment was being used, and he was quick to voice his objections. He wrote in his diary:

> The General Staff is now trying to run the Air Service with just as much knowledge of it as a hog knows about skating. It is terrible to have to fight with an organization of this kind, instead of devoting all our attention to the powerful enemy on our front.

The Germans lost one of their best leaders on July 3, when Wilhelm Reinhardt, with twenty victories, was killed in a flying accident. During the period he had led *Jasta 11*, the group scored 177 confirmed victories. He was replaced by Erich Lowenhardt, who immediately combined *Jastas 10* and *11*.

At this point the Allies needed every man and every airplane, but on July 10 they lost an entire flight of six Bréguets from the 96th Aero Squadron in a mission that William Mitchell called "the most disgraceful performance in the war." Under the command of Major Brown, the Bréguets went out with a strong tailwind, climbing high above the clouds that closed in on them. They finally came down through a hole in the overcast and saw a city that none of the pilots recognized. They were deep in Germany—so far behind the lines that one by one the Bréguets ran out of fuel as they tried to fly home against the headwind. All six planes made forced landings in enemy territory, and the crews were captured.

A few days later a German fighter dropped a note on the American field. It said, "Thanks for the six planes, but what shall we do with the major?"

After this episode the squadron's operations report read: "Army bombardment, First Day Bombardment Group, 96th Aero Squadron: Planes on hand, 2; available for duty, 1."

But all the news for the Americans was not bad. During the first four weeks they were in the Château-Thierry sector, they were credited with thirty-eight confirmed victories while losing thirty-six. They were matched against the toughest and most experienced German pilots, yet they had more than held their own.

Meanwhile, another competition had been held in Germany for single-seat fighters. Fokker again came away the winner, this time with a monoplane, his first successful design of this type since the old E-4. The new machine was first designated E-5, but this was changed to D-8. There was no legitimate reason for this latter designation, since as a monoplane (*eindecker*) it should have been designated in the E-class rather than the D (*doppledecker*, or biplane).

Slightly smaller than the D-7, which it was to replace, the new machine was faster than its predecessor, with a maximum speed of 127 miles per hour at sea level. It could also climb faster, reaching 3,280 feet in two minutes and 10,000 feet in slightly under nine minutes. Absolute ceiling was 22,100 feet.

Hermann Goering once said that the Fokker D-7 gave the German airmen "a new lease on life." It is probable that the

D-8 would have made them still more formidable if it had not been for official bungling, which prevented the machine from arriving at the fighting fronts in quantity. As it was, only a comparatively few examples were received by the *jastas*. However, the mere presence of the airplane indicated that as late as July 1918 the Germans were preparing for a longer war.

The test was still going to be crucial. Allied leaders were not quite sure when the massed German armies would strike, but they did know that the major burden of fighting would fall on the Americans. The British and French infantrymen were as close to exhaustion as they could be without total collapse. If defeat was to be avoided, this had to be done by the fresh troops from across the Atlantic.

Fokker's last fighter plane of the war was the D-8 monoplane, which was planned as replacement for the D-7. Only a few D-8's reached the front before the Armistice.   *Peter M. Bowers*

Thunder Along the Front

Chapter Thirteen

"I SHALL NEVER FORGET July 15, 1918, as long as I live," Major Harold Hartney wrote. "It seemed as if the whole German army, in desperation, simply hurled itself at our part of the lines around Château-Thierry. Our boys were in the air practically all the time. Frantic orders came through asking us, high-flying pursuit planes, to skim the ground and try to fix the position and extent of the German advance. It was the ultimate of frenzied excitement. Allied troops of all kinds were rushing by us in both directions, French going back on relief, waves of Americans going forward. It was the climax of the war."

By the following morning the Allied position appeared extremely serious. The Germans had broken through and were literally pouring across the Marne.

The enemy enjoyed aerial superiority over this grim battlefield, and the Allies had gone to all lengths to send out observation planes to seek vital information. On one occasion, to provide protection from German formations of from fifteen to twenty fighters, a total of ninety-six American machines went up to protect a single observation plane!

According to Major L. H. Brereton, who was in charge of American attack operations, this was the closest the United States ever came to its threat to blacken the skies with droves of airplanes. "However," he added, "none of these were American airplanes, although the aviators were Americans."

During this trying period Colonel Mitchell made a spectacular flight, which is not often mentioned by writers chronicling feats of heroism in the war. Mitchell was aware that if this huge German push was successful Paris would undoubtedly be captured; and if Paris fell, the French armies would collapse. He also knew that the average flyer did not know enough about military tactics and strategy to read the full meaning of troop movements on the ground. It was of extreme importance that an assessment of the situation be made by someone who would understand the full implications of the infantry situation; he decided to go himself without requesting permission from his superiors, knowing that such a request would be turned down.

Completely alone and with no protection, Colonel Mitchell took off in a Nieuport before daybreak and flew straight to the lines, where he followed the course of the Marne. He saw a few Fokkers in the vicinity of Jaulgonne, but the enemy pilots either did not see him or chose to ignore him. He went down to 500 feet and continued his lone reconnaissance. All of the bridges across the Marne had been reported destroyed, but Mitchell saw that east of Dormans, approximately at the middle of the salient, the Germans had thrown up five pontoon bridges, and that enemy troops were streaming across these bridges by the thousands. This information had not been reported back to Army Headquarters, even though it was of vital importance.

"This flight by a pursuit plane and the resulting information was, I think, unquestionably one of the greatest flights of the entire war," Major Elmer Haslett wrote. "I did not learn until several days later who the aviator was. No one seemed to know, nor could we find any record on the regular reports."

When Colonel Mitchell returned from his amazing flight he had already worked out a plan of action. He immediately proposed that the pontoon bridges be bombed and that the huge German supply base at Fère-en-Tardenois be hit with everything the Allies could muster. At the same time, he suggested that if the Germans could be attacked in the rear, either at Soissons or Reims, it might be possible to destroy their entire attacking army. Marshal Ferdinand Foch, who had been appointed Supreme Commander of all Allied forces on April 15, 1918, saw the value of the plan and quickly ordered it into operation.

This was the turning point of the war. There would still be much fighting ahead, but Colonel Mitchell's solo flight at great personal risk had at last given the Allies a plan through which they could win.

This plan developed into the largest combined aerial and ground operation the Americans had attempted to that time. In addition to the American planes, the British sent in several squadrons attached to the new Independent Air Force, which had been organized by General Trenchard.

At noon on July 16 this aerial armada struck with its full force. It bombed ammunition dumps and supply depots, strafed troops, and blew up the Marne bridges. The enemy troops that had crossed the river were cut off both from supplies and an avenue of retreat.

While the airplanes were busy, Allied troops were moved toward Soissons and Reims in strength. These movements were made at night, so that enemy aerial observers would not see what was being planned, while during the day other troops were dispatched in the opposite direction.

The Allied armies struck on the morning of July 18, hitting Soissons and Reims simultaneously. Meanwhile, Mitchell sent his airmen into the fray in concentrated formations. During that single day the pilots went out time and again, coming back only to refuel and have their ammunition and bomb supplies replenished. Some of the men flew as many as twenty hours, munching quick snacks while their planes were being serviced.

"No man ever saw a more magnificent or, rather, a more significant sight," one of the pilots wrote about a patrol. "Here was the tide of a world war involving twenty million men actually turning before my very eyes. Our Doughboys, fresh, vigorous, and engaging in their first major battle, were sweeping across the Marne, outflanking the famous Prussian Guard and actually setting it back on its heels."

The Germans were being pushed back, but the aerial cost was high. Major Reginald Maxwell led his Independent Air Force squadrons against the enemy ammunition dump at Fère-en-Tardenois and reduced it to ruin, but he said he lost "literally dozens of planes." The Americans also lost eight men and planes in nine days. But it was the French who supported the operation with the largest number of aircraft and who also suffered the heaviest casualties. Of the 518 Allied planes that fell in battle that month, the majority wore French markings.

While the French planes and pilots took the brunt of the German attacks, they also scored impressive victories. During July the irrepressible René Fonck ran his total to fifty-six confirmed victories, including doubles on the 15th and 19th of the month and a treble on the 18th. Fonck spent hours developing himself into the finest aerial marksman of the war, and in some notable cases he required only five or six bullets from his rapid-fire weapons to dispose of an enemy. In commenting on his marksmanship, he once said, "I put my bullets into the target as if I placed them there by hand."

Then, on July 28, Edward Mannock was killed. When the final scores were added up at the end of the war, Mannock was listed as the highest British ace, with seventy-three confirmed victories.

If ever there was an enigma in the fighting skies of World War I, it was Mannock. He became a pilot on November 28, 1916, and went into combat for the first time in a Nieuport the following April. He was not known as a particularly good pilot or even a particularly good marksman. He was also nearly blind in one eye. But while Mannock seemed to lack all the attributes usually required for an outstanding war flyer, he had two unusual facets in his make-up: dogged perseverance and total hatred for the enemy.

Mannock's hatred for Germans was almost an obsession. He wanted to do more than just destroy the enemy's aircraft: he took personal satisfaction out of killing. On more than one occasion he turned his machine guns on enemy airmen who managed to escape from their crashed machines, trying to cut them down on the ground. This was strictly against the code of ethics followed by most pilots on both sides.

Just as Mannock had little regard for the enemy, so his squadron-mates in the beginning of his career as a war flyer had little respect for him. In fact, many considered him a coward. During April 1917, while his squadron lost half its strength in desperate fighting, Mannock somehow managed to come through without a single bullet hole in his airplane. The squadron log for that month carried the accusing line, "Mannock—forty hours patrol over the lines—no combats." During that same month another new pilot, who reached the front only a week before Mannock, scored twelve victories. His name was William Bishop.

Mannock was very close to being transferred to the rear areas, if not indeed disgraced by court-martial, when on May 7, 1917—the day Albert Ball was killed—he finally scored. A full month went by before he added another German to his record. Then, suddenly, he was a different man and victories came rapidly. By the end of 1917 his record stood at twenty-three.

As a result of this performance, Mannock was made a flight leader of No. 74 Squadron, which was equipped with S.E.5's. He soon became known as one of the greatest flight leaders of the war. One of his pilots wrote, "Flying with Mannock is perfectly safe. His leadership is foolproof."

Mannock now had respect as a pilot and a leader, but still he was not liked by many as a person, primarily because of his attitude toward the enemy. When Baron von Richthofen was killed, one of the members of Mannock's squadron proposed a toast to the gallant German. Mannock was the only man in the room who refused to participate in the toast. Instead, he was quoted as saying, "I hope he roasted all the way down."

The story is also told about a British journalist who tore up his notes after interviewing Mannock for a newspaper feature. "The man is a monster," the journalist purportedly said. "The Germans would be justified in considering us barbarians if they could hear him talk!"

Despite his hatred of Germans, no flight leader could have been a better teacher or protector than Mannock was of his own men. It is known that he intentionally gave several of his victories to members of his flight to bolster their courage and morale.

After some three months with No. 74 Squadron, Mannock was transferred to No. 85 Squadron. He was also promoted to major. On the day of his final flight, he went up with Lieutenant D.C. Inglis, who had not yet scored. The two S.E.5a's left their drome at dawn on July 26.

The British pilots flew over the lines to Merville, where they encountered a German two-seater. Operating by prearranged plan, Mannock dived beneath the enemy and then zoomed, firing from below, while Inglis came down at it from above. The German plane fell in flames, and both S.E.5a's followed, still shooting. They were now low over enemy territory, and suddenly Mannock's machine burst into flames. No one knows exactly how it happened. His fighter could have been hit by ground fire or by the gunner in the rear seat of the German plane before it crashed, or it could have caught fire from a broken fuel line or some other malfunction.

When Inglis returned to his drome, he said, "I could see a small flame and some smoke flickering out from the right side of the plane. Round and round it went until it hit the ground near some trenches. On impact it burst into flames. I flew around to see if he was all right, but he never left his plane."

Edward Mannock was awarded the Victoria Cross posthumously, with the following citation:

This highly distinguished officer, during the whole of his career in the Royal Air Force, was an outstanding example of fearless courage, remarkable skill, devotion to duty and self-sacrifice, which has never been surpassed.

July 31 was a bad day for the Americans. Lieutenant John McArthur of the 27th Squadron led his flight out to strafe the Richthofen *jasta,* which had moved from Coincy to the airdrome north of Fismes. Only one of the six returned. Two of the pilots were killed, while three others were forced down when their fuel was exhausted. That same day Alan Winslow, the first American to win a victory, was killed in combat.

The following day eighteen Americans went out in formation to protect two French Salmson photographic planes. Five of the fighters did not return. One pilot who did get back was Lieutenant O.T. Beauchamp, who was on his first flight over the lines. His combat report gives a classic example of the unstable characteristics of the Nieuport 28:

We were attacked by eight Fokker biplanes east of Fère-en-Tardenois. I tried to bank to the left and fell into a spin. When I came out of the spin there were four enemy aircraft on my tail. I tried to turn again but fell into another spin. I was followed by the four enemy aircraft down to 3,000 feet. As I was coming out of the spin a Boche machine was headed straight at me. I fired and he turned to the left. I turned a little to the left and turned back again. Being right on his tail I fired about twenty bullets into him. He fell off slowly on his right wing and went into a spin. I turned on the other machines and went into a spin. When I came out they were climbing up. . . .

Despite his unintentional aerobatics, Beauchamp claimed three victories. Not one of these was confirmed.

Two other pilots who went out that day on their first combat patrols were Frank Luke and Joseph Wehner. Within two months these two, flying as a team, were to score an amazing number of victories. Within two months both would also be dead.

On August 2 a patrol of eighteen airplanes from the 135th Aero Squadron took off from the drome at Ourches and pointed

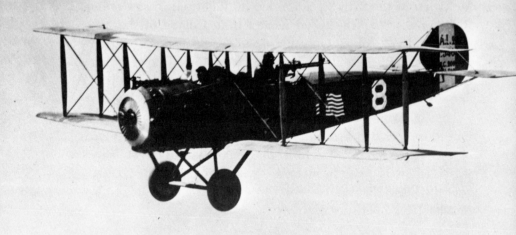

A French Salmson in American colors. The U.S. Air Service ordered more Salmsons than any other foreign two-seaters; 705 were delivered, of which 557 were flown in combat. *U.S. Air Force*

for the lines. The planes were D.H.4's—the first American-built aircraft to go into action. These were almost immediately dubbed "flaming coffins" by their crews, and a great hue and cry went up in the United States about the quality of equipment being furnished to its fighting men.

There was practically nothing to commend the American-built D.H.4, although some writers have attempted to justify it. In its original form, the plane was a misfit, a combination of mistakes from nose to tail. Major Harold Hartney called it "a very disgraceful compromise between a budding good engine, the Liberty, and the English Corps Observation plane, the D.H." This was not a condemnation of American industry, but rather lack of wartime knowledge at that point.

The first mistake in the D.H.4, as acknowledged later, had been that of trying to adapt a foreign aircraft to the Liberty engine instead of designing a plane around the engine. (Better still, a foreign engine should have been selected for U.S. manufacture. The Liberty finally developed into an excellent engine—one of the world's best—but not until 286 changes had been made after the war.) The landing-gear arrangement of the D.H.4 was bad, giving the ship a tendency to nose over on soft or muddy fields, and the three-section fuselage construction caused the machine to come apart too easily. In an effort to counteract the nose-heavy condition, some observers even climbed out of their cockpits and crawled back on the fuselage during landings!

An unidentified member of the First Day Bombardment Group wrote a short history of his outfit, in which he commented on the D.H.4 in these words:

Some idea of how far it fell short of expectations can be formed when it is known that the bomb racks were constructed to hold ten bombs, and though at first it was attempted to fly with four, it was subsequently necessary to cut the number to two. The machines were also without the armored seats then in fairly frequent use. . . . In such antiquated machines these boys were asked daily to face death.

Personnel of the U.S. Air Service 11th Aero Squadron, Day Bombardment, with their D.H.4's. The planes were called "flaming coffins"
because they caught fire so readily.   *U.S. Air Force*

Perhaps the greatest problem with the D.H.4 was the location of its fuel tank, which was in the fuselage between the pilot and observer. With the heavy tank behind him, the pilot was an almost certain fatality in any crash. It was also said that the machine often caught fire without assistance from the enemy.

Captain Rickenbacker described one combat he observed in which D.H.4's were engaged:

> From every side Fokkers were piquing upon the clumsy Liberty machines which, with their criminally constructed fuel tanks, offered so easy a target to the incendiary bullets of the enemy that their unfortunate pilots called this boasted achievement of our Aviation Department their "flaming coffins." During that one brief fight over Grand Pré, I saw three of these crude machines go down in flames, an American pilot and an American gunner in each "flaming coffin" dying this frightful and needless death.

These faults were corrected in the D.H.4B. But while 1,213 D.H.4's were shipped from the United States to France before the Armistice, not one of the improved D.H.4B's arrived.

On August 8 the entire First Pursuit Group had its Nieuport 28's replaced by Spad S-13's. Some of the American pilots considered this a blessing, while others called it a catastrophe.

Many of the pilots loved the tricky Nieuports, but others feared them. In truth, both the Nieuport and Spad were inferior to British fighters then in service. The French themselves had ordered the Nieuport 28 only in limited numbers, but 298 were obtained by the Americans. The United States bought 189 Spad S-7's and 893 S-13's. Another 2,000 S-13's were ordered from the Curtiss company, but this contract was canceled after the Armistice.

In spite of the frailty of the Nieuport, it was an excellent fighting machine and very sensitive to the controls. Equally important, it was easy to service because of its rotary engine. The Spad, while stronger, was not nearly as maneuverable and its Hispano-Suiza engine was not considered dependable.

With their highly maneuverable Fokker D-7's, the Germans shot down Allied planes as never before. One *jagdstaffel* alone claimed 81 victories in a single week.   *U.S. Air Force*

It was called a "monster" to service. As a result of the servicing problems, the number of aircraft available for operations on any one day dropped from about 90 percent to 50 percent.

On the same day that the Spads arrived at the American field, the British started a drive into the German lines around Amiens. The enemy was suffering badly in the Château-Thierry sector, and the Amiens push was made to take advantage of the situation. The R.A.F. concentrated 1,390 aircraft on this front against a German force of between 340 and 360.

The British airmen went out in formations sometimes numbering as many as sixty-five planes. Hundreds of attacks were made against ground targets, including enemy flying fields. The Germans had never before been subjected to a more ferocious or concentrated offensive, and they were forced to fall back. Their lines of retreat were across the Somme bridges. The British knew that if they could destroy these bridges the enemy would be faced with a major disaster. However, this was one time when airpower failed to do its job. Two hundred and five bombing attacks were made in broad daylight against the bridges, and not a single span was broken.

The Germans were outnumbered about four to one in the air, yet their pilots did not turn and flee. They pointed their guns at the British squadrons and fought bravely. On the first day of the attack, the R.A.F. lost forty-five planes in combat while fifty-two others were destroyed through combat damage. This amounted to 13 percent of the aircraft actually sent into action and 7 percent of the entire operational force concentrated in the sector. Most of these victories were scored by German pilots flying the Fokker D-7.

The R.A.F. losses were so heavy because the Germans quickly moved *Jagdgeschwader 1* up from Fismes to help stem the attack. That day the hunting group made fifty-nine sorties. Ernst Udet, Erich Loewenhardt, and Lothar von Richthofen alone claimed eight victories among them that day, while the following day this formidable trio accounted for another eleven.

On August 10 Loewenhardt was killed. He was at that time the highest-scoring surviving German, with fifty-four victories. But he did not die in combat. Instead, he was killed as Boelcke had been: in a midair collision. This time the second party to the collision was Lieutenant Wentz, a new pilot to the outfit, who managed to escape by parachute. The Germans had just recently started issuing parachutes, but Loewenhardt tried to bring his ship under control instead of jumping. When he finally jumped, he was at only 300 feet. The parachute did not open in time.

While the German troops were being struck heavy blows in all sectors, the British Independent Air Force began to hit the rear areas.

The Independent Air Force was established entirely through the efforts of one man, General Sir Hugh Trenchard. In April 1918, when the Allies were still on the brink of disaster and praying for the Americans to arrive, Trenchard went before Parliament and insisted that the Germans had missed their greatest opportunity of the war when they failed to press their bombing raids against England. Had they continued, he said, it would have been necessary to withdraw large numbers of airplanes and antiaircraft guns from France. At the same time, they could have disrupted British morale and also damaged, if not ruined, war-production facilities. For these reasons, he requested permission to organize an air force that would be free to select its own objectives, aided by intelligence reports, and operate strategically as opposed to the tactical use the French made of their bombing force. This meant, simply, that Trenchard proposed to use his air force against the enemy rear areas rather than in conjunction with the troops. The General said:

> The war can drag on indefinitely if we continue to hurl our weight against the German army in the field. It can be won quickly by striking at the heart of that army through a relentless attack on its sources of supply.
>
> We have to have both day and night bombardment squadrons.

It is necessary that the enemy must always fear attack during all the twenty-four hours. If he does, he has to concentrate men and equipment constantly to repel attacks that may come to him at any hour. To tie up so much equipment and so many men in defense against possible attack is almost as great a feat as to destroy those men and that equipment.

This was the most advanced airpower thinking that had ever been suggested, and Parliament quickly gave General Trenchard permission to organize his Independent Air Force, which came into being officially on June 5, 1918. It never grew beyond the strength of ten squadrons, but its value went far beyond the number of aircraft employed. The crews were all volunteers, and they were warned in advance that they were taking on the most dangerous flying tasks in the war.

Trenchard's air force carried out fifty-seven long-distance raids against German cities, including Cologne and Stuttgart. It struck against Gotha airdromes, railroads, and Rhineland chemical factories. Though it inflicted considerable damage on German war industry, its most powerful effect was on the morale of the people.

During its operational life of five months, the Independent Air Force dropped 540 tons of bombs on enemy industrial centers and flying fields, flew 11,784 hours, fired 353,260 rounds of ammunition, and destroyed 150 German airplanes in combat. Its own losses were listed as 111 aircraft.

The German infantrymen were being pushed back all along the line, but they were not giving ground easily. Major Harold Hartney told in his remarkable book *Up and at 'Em* about the sight of one of the battlefields after the war had passed on. He wrote:

Never have my eyes rested on such a sight. May they never again behold one like it. The hill was literally covered with dead men, side by side, head to head, little or no space between, practically all of them American Doughboys. They had died in droves charging German machine gun nests left behind to cover the retreat.

Right in front of us were a German and an American who had actually pierced each other with their bayonets and neither bayonet had been withdrawn.

That same month, even while they were losing, the Germans shot 565 Allied aircraft out of the skies and caused uncounted others to be discarded as worthless. They were sturdy foes who were willing to settle their own war whether the ground forces won or lost.

Beginning of the End

Chapter Fourteen

THE GERMANS ON THE BRITISH FRONT had been driven back to
the Hindenburg Line once again. Their deep penetrations
made in the offensive starting March 21 had been completely
wiped out. They had come close to success, and they had failed,
being pushed back to the same trenches they had occupied a
year earlier.

The enemy flyers abandoned the last vestige of their previous cautious tactics. They were greatly outnumbered in most
sectors, but they no longer attempted to conserve their airplanes. The Allies had to be stopped no matter what the cost.
Two airmen in a Hannover, Major Guenther and Lieutenant
Schweiffeger, even came down low enough to fight it out with
two tanks near Vraucort. They destroyed one of the tanks with
machine-gun fire, then directed artillery shoots on the other
until it was also knocked out of action.

On September 2 Bruno Loerzer proved what the hunting
groups could do. He took *Jagdgeschwader 3* out over Arras and
put on two of the greatest dogfights of the war, with results
that were incredibly lopsided. In these two engagements, a full
twenty-six British airplanes were shot down without a single
German loss. Loerzer explained the action in his combat report:

We made three flights this day, the first between 9 and 11 A.M., the second between 11 A.M. and 1 P.M., and the last between 5 and 7 P.M. Bad weather. *J.G. 3* had about thirty aircraft in the air flying in closed formation at about 1,500 feet [he may have meant 15,000 feet, which seems more likely] when a British unit flying in open order was noticed. As a result of our tight formation attack there were twelve enemy aircraft destroyed without loss to ourselves. At the second attack we had an experienced enemy who attacked from a greater height and we thought we were lost, but it proved otherwise and we destroyed fourteen "Tommies." Our two successes must have made an impression on the other side, for our third patrol could not find any of our enemy, so I decided to support our hardfighting infantry.

General von Hindenburg wrote a personal commendation to the unit:

I beg *J.G. 3* to accept my full congratulations for twenty-six successful combats without loss on September 2nd. The behavior of its commander, Lieutenant Loerzer, and of his decision when he did not find opponents in the air to take action against troops and tanks, is an example to all.

Meanwhile, something of major importance was brewing. As far back as July 24, the decision had been made to attack the strong German salient at St. Mihiel. The operation was to be almost entirely American—fifteen U.S. divisions and only four French colonial divisions. The troops were to be supported by 2,900 cannon and 400 tanks, with the entire force concentrated along a front of only about thirty miles.

Late in August Colonel William Mitchell met in Bar-le-Duc with Major Hartney, commander of the First Pursuit Group. Mitchell said he wanted the group to move up to a new field at Rembercourt in preparation for the offensive, though warning that the field was quite small, comprising only thirty acres.

"Our boys can land their Spads on a dime," Major Hartney replied, "and if there are small hills, so much the better, regardless of wind direction."

This small flying group was only a part of Mitchell's command for the offensive. He actually had the largest number of aircraft ever assembled for any one operation. These were composed of forty-nine British and American squadrons plus forty French *escadrilles*. In addition, there were nine squadrons from the Independent Air Force. The aggregate total was 1,481 aircraft, all of which were under Mitchell's direct control with the exception of the Independent Air Force, which was to operate under his advice but not direct instructions. This broke down to 701 fighters, 366 observation planes, 323 day bombers, and ninety-one night bombers.

The St. Mihiel drive opened on September 12 with a four-hour artillery bombardment, after which some 500,000 American troops surged forward from their trenches. In support of the ground action, Mitchell formed two attack brigades of about 400 airplanes each, with the remainder held in reserve or on standby for special duty. One of these brigades was ordered to confine its activities to a stretch of front measuring only twelve miles. The object was to force the enemy to send his air strength out to defend that sector. Meanwhile, the other brigade was scheduled to hit from the opposite side of the salient, with its attention directed against the rear area.

The bombers made strategic attacks against railroad centers, troop concentrations, and communications systems. They also joined the fighters by participating in tactical operations: observing, photographing, directing artillery fire, and strafing troops and supply lines. Lieutenant James Knowles was one of the American pilots involved in the huge operation. His combat report read:

Found German artillery and wagon trains retreating on the road Crue-Vigneulles. Flying at about ten meters [approximately thirty-eight feet] attacked and killed several horses in wagon train. Others ran away and piled up among the artillery, causing great confusion and blocking the road. Artillery horses ran away and all piled up in one big heap. Vigneulles on fire and big explosion occurred about 6:10 P.M. Heavy machine-gun fire from the ground. No enemy aircraft sighted.

Raymond Collinshaw in the cockpit of his Sopwith Camel. A Canadian, Collishaw scored 60 victories, placing him third in the Royal Air Force's final tally sheet.

An airman's view of Vaux, France, which was destroyed by American artillery and aerial bombardment. This had been German-occupied territory for more than two years. *U.S. Air Force*

The German infantry, outnumbered and outfought, was forced back, and the retreat was harassed virtually every foot of the way. The fleeing troops choked the roads, and they were bombed and strafed throughout the day until night fell. The American pilots flew long hours, returning to their dromes only long enough to refuel and load up with ammunition and bombs before they made another low-level dash across the lines.

That day the 11th and 20th Aero Squadrons of the First Day Bombardment Group were sent into the battle to undertake reconnaissance, and also to act as two-seat fighters on *escort* to the Spads of the First Pursuit Group! However, when it was demonstrated that the lumbering D.H.4's could not keep up with the Spads, let alone protect them, they were reassigned to their proper work of day bombing.

On the morning of August 13, the 20th Squadron went out in formation. These were the first American-built airplanes to drop bombs on the enemy. The entire squadron returned without loss.

The battle continued, but then strong opposition appeared from several German *staffels,* including *Jagdgeswader* 2 under Oskar von Boenigk. *J.G.* 2 destroyed eighty-one Allied planes in the St. Mihiel operation while losing but two of its own. One of the Allied groups receiving the brunt of Fokker fire was the 11th Aero Squadron. On September 14 it lost two planes, and the following day out of a formation of six D.H.4's that crossed the lines, only one managed to limp back, its wings and fuselage riddled with bullet holes. That same day the 96th Squadron lost four planes.

But while the two-seaters were being mauled, only three casualties were suffered by the First Pursuit Group. The official records show that the group was credited with thirty-four victories from September 12 to 26.

The Spads might have scored even more heavily if they had not had trouble with their guns. The Americans were using .30-caliber ammunition, whereas the standard French ammunition was .303 caliber. Aircraft supplied by the factories were fitted with ammunition boxes for French ammunition, and these did not take the U.S.-made ammunition properly. The Marlin guns on the American planes were also troublesome, often jamming after only a few rounds had been fired. In some cases this left the pilots completely defenseless in the midst of battle. They tried to bluff it out by flying ferociously at the enemy, but when the pretense no longer worked, they broke off combat and sped to their home bases.

The St. Mihiel battle was short and surprisingly successful. Casualties were far lower than had been anticipated. The Allies lost about 7,000 men, while approximately 15,000 German prisoners were taken. The salient was also completely removed. But even more important, Colonel Mitchell had learned that his employment of airpower had worked out exactly as he had hoped and anticipated. The airplane as a weapon was finally reaching full maturity. The United States, which had entered the war in fourteenth place among the world aviation powers, was able to provide advanced air strategy even if she could not supply superior aircraft.

After the St. Mihiel front had been consolidated, the American ground and air units moved into the Meuse-Argonne sector for the next offensive. The number of Allied airplanes available for this operation was considerably smaller—about 800—but the ratio of American planes had increased to approximately 600. More than 1,200,000 American troops were concentrated for the battle, of which about half were committed to combat while the others were held in reserve. As at St. Mihiel, General Pershing also had several French divisions under his command.

At the same time, farther north, the British and French, with American assistance, were preparing another offensive. This meant that the entire central and northern sections of the enemy lines were to be hit in coordinated attacks.

The line on which the Germans were making their stand was the most formidable system of trenches and fortifications of the entire war. The Hindenburg Line had been built carefully, and the Germans considered it virtually impregnable. It consisted of a network of trenches and strong points five miles deep, plus a wide canal studded with concrete shelters and machine-gun pillboxes. There was also a tunnel nearly three miles long, which was deep enough and strong enough to withstand any bombardment and protect the soldiers inside.

None of the Allied commanders tried to fool themselves. The job ahead of them was formidable, and they knew that losses would be extremely heavy. They also knew that if the Hindenburg Line could be broken, the Germans would have to surrender.

So great was the demand for secrecy before the battle that the first American observation flights over the Meuse-Argonne sector were in old French planes so the Germans would not know that American troops were in the sector. These flights were kept at a very low level because of extremely bad weather, including rain, fog, and high winds.

Because of the poor weather, the Germans were putting their faith in observation balloons along this stretch of the front. American headquarters considered the balloons a menace and asked William Mitchell, who had now been promoted to brigadier general, to have them destroyed.

The battle started before dawn on September 26 with an artillery barrage that illuminated the sky to the brilliance of daylight all along the sector. "The German batteries were drawn up along their front scarcely a mile back of their lines," Rickenbacker wrote. "And on our side a vastly more crowded line of flashes indicated the overwhelming superiority in numbers of guns that the American artillerymen were using."

A selected group of pilots flew above this gigantic battlefield, their objective the German balloons. Within an hour six of the balloons had been sent blazing to the ground. The First Pursuit Group also brought down two Fokkers without losing a single plane or pilot of their own.

But while the fighters came through with low casualties, the

Ernst Udet in front of his Fokker D-7. Udet scored 62 victories, the last two of which were over American D.H.4's. He was the top-ranking living German ace at the end of the war.

William Goepel

two-seaters were badly hurt. The 20th Aero Squadron sent out a formation of seven planes and only two of these returned, one with a dead observer. And this was only one squadron. During the day virtually all the two-seater units suffered heavy losses. An entire formation of D.H.4's fell to Ernst Udet's *jasta*, two of these going down under the guns of the leader himself.

The following day, September 27, the attack was started on the Flanders front. The British had approximately 1,000 airplanes on their sector, while the French and American squadrons had an even larger number. The Germans were outnumbered on the ground and in the air as never before.

Two days later Frank Luke was killed. In only seventeen days he was credited with destroying fourteen enemy balloons and four airplanes.

Luke was an enigma to the other pilots from the day he joined the 27th Aero Squadron. He went out on his first patrol August 1, and while he continued to fly regularly, he somehow managed to miss the action. Then on August 16 he claimed his first victory, but this was never confirmed. Most of his squadron-mates, who disliked Luke, doubted the story. Luke rarely mixed with the other pilots, preferring to be left alone. He had a record of insubordination and hostility to authority. After the incident of the claimed victory, he was considered a liar and was despised by the other pilots, with three exceptions. One of these was Joseph Wehner.

Luke and Wehner made a natural pair. They were both quiet and withdrawn, and both were of German parentage. Wehner had even been investigated by the Secret Service because of suspected sympathies for Germany. He had been suspect not only because of his background, but because prior to the United States entry into the war he had been doing Y.M.C.A. relief work in the prison camps in Germany.

Luke and Wehner formed a team to attack enemy balloons, which was considered the most dangerous type of combat flying. Because of the extreme importance of these aerial observation posts, the balloons were heavily defended from below by machine guns and antiaircraft guns, while German airplanes often protected them from above. Luke and Wehner set up a system whereby Luke would go down after a balloon, while Wehner protected him from above.

Frank Luke's first confirmed victory came on September 12 when he set fire to a balloon at Marrieulles. This time he wanted to make sure that no one doubted his story, so he landed near an American balloon company that had seen the action and had them sign as witnesses. But while he had finally scored, his Spad was so riddled with bullets that it had to be scrapped. This was the first of five airplanes he brought back from combat so filled with holes that they had to be discarded, while Wehner had three Spads virtually shot from under him.

On September 14 Luke knocked down two more balloons, while Wehner went after two Fokkers and destroyed one of them.

After this incident Lieutenant Leo Dawson exclaimed enthusiastically, "If anybody still thinks Luke is yellow, he's crazy. He's not yellow; he's stark, raving mad. He went by me on that attack like a wild man. I thought he was diving right into the balloon. Then, after it was blazing, I saw him take another swoop down on it!"

Even with these successes, Luke and Wehner were not satisfied. Flushed with victory, they told the mechanics to service their riddled Spads for another flight. However, Captain Alfred Grant, Commanding Officer of the 27th Squadron, insisted that Luke stay on the ground. "He's making a burlesque of the 27th," Grant said, "and I'm not going to stand for it. Balloons or no balloons, we must have discipline."

Joe Wehner was given permission to go out alone, his objective the German balloon at Waroq. René Fonck destroyed the balloon just minutes before Wehner arrived, but the audacious American dived into a formation of eight Fokkers that was attacking an observation plane. He shot down one of the enemy machines and forced another one down out of control.

Continuing their frenetic pace, Luke and Wehner piled victory on top of victory. But the pace could not continue indefinitely. On September 18 Joe Wehner died.

On that day the two Americans, flying together as usual, destroyed a pair of balloons. After getting his, Wehner climbed up again, just in time to see a flight of Fokkers sweeping down after Luke. Wehner fired a Very pistol in warning, but Luke did not see the flare. In a desperate effort to save his friend, Wehner went after the enemy planes. However, the odds were too great.

Joe Wehner was killed attempting to save Luke, when he could easily have escaped. It is ironic that while Wehner was known to have scored eight times, the official list of victorious American airmen issued following the war gave him credit for only five balloons and no airplanes. This is especially confusing inasmuch as the official citation with his Distinguished Service Cross acknowledged that he destroyed an enemy machine on September 15 and forced another down out of control.

After Wehner fell, Frank Luke turned on the Fokkers and sent two of them crashing. Then, his fuel tank almost empty, he broke away. On his way home he saw three French Spads attacking an L.V.G. two-seater at long range. The American raced past the French planes and destroyed the L.V.G.

Luke had scored five victories in less than ten minutes—two balloons and three airplanes. He had now passed Rickenbacker as the highest-scoring American.

Frank Luke wrote his last combat report on September 28. It read:

I flew north to Verdun, crossed the lines at about 500 meters [1,640 feet] and found a balloon in its nest in the region of Bethenville. I dove on it firing both guns. After I pulled away it burst into flames. As I could not find any others I returned to the airdrome. One confirmation requested.

Luke flew out again the following day and did not return. There were no American observers to his last flight. However, the story was told in detail in the following sworn statement:

> The undersigned, living in Murvaux, Department of the Meuse, certify to have seen on the 29th of September, 1918, toward evening an American aviator followed by an *escadrille* of Germans in the direction of Liny, descend suddenly and vertically toward the earth, then straighten out close to the ground and fly in direction of Briers Farm, where he found a German captive balloon which he burned. Then he flew toward Milly where he found another balloon which he also burned in spite of incessant fire directed toward his machine. There he apparently was wounded by a shot from rapid fire cannon. From there he came back over Murvaux and still with his guns he killed six German soldiers and wounded as many more.
>
> Following this he landed and got out of his machine, undoubtedly to quench his thirst at the stream. He had gone fifty yards when seeing the Germans come toward him still had the strength to draw his revolver to defend himself. A moment after he fell dead following a serious wound he received in the chest.

The Graves Registration section of the U.S. Army located the pilot's body where it had been buried by the people of Murvaux, and it was identified as Frank Luke. But none of the men who knew him had required this proof; the description of his final flight and actions on the ground had been sufficient identification. Frank Luke had lived, flown, and fought as a maverick; he had died the same way.

There was no longer any doubt over the outcome of the war. The Germans were beaten, and it was just a matter of time before the entire military machine collapsed. But this was not because of lack of will to resist by the airmen, for in the final stages of the war they fought as never before. In September, for example, they brought down 773 Allied aircraft—the largest number destroyed in any single month of the war and higher than the entire total of 1916.

On October 9 the American Air Service conducted its heaviest raid of the war. More than 350 bombers and fighters under General Mitchell went out in two formations to bomb and strafe a large concentration of infantrymen who had been gathered for a counterattack. More than thirty tons of bombs were dropped, and casualties were so heavy among the German troops and their morale so shaken that the attack was canceled.

Mitchell was so pleased with the results that he called the operation "the dawn of the day when great air forces will be capable of definitely affecting a ground decision on the field of battle."

The German airmen continued fighting with complete dedication to their cause, even while their ground forces were being pushed back farther and farther. Evidence of this fighting spirit was reflected in the action on October 30. That single day the Germans lost sixty-seven aircraft while bringing down forty-one British planes.

An official French communiqué issued on November 5 indicated how fiercely the Germans were fighting. It read:

> During the fighting in the month of October, our antiaircraft defense force took an important part in the fighting against German aircraft. The mission of the latter was to cover the retreat of the enemy troops and to impede our advance. They showed themselves particularly aggressive, machine-gunning our infantry and our batteries. Thanks to the excellence of their shooting, their skill, and the vigilance of the personnel, our antiaircraft formations largely contributed to levying a high price upon the enemy for his daring tactics. Thirty-five German aeroplanes were brought down by our posts and our auto cannon and four machines were so damaged that they were obliged to abandon their mission.
>
> Special mention is due to the 68th Section of auto-cannon of the 66th Regiment of Artillery, over which a patrol of five Fokkers flew at a low altitude. A veritable battle ensued. The coolness of the gunners under a rain of bombs and machine-gun bullets, enabled the gunners to bring down in a few minutes three machines, while a fourth, fleeing before a murderous fire, fell to the ground after being hit by the fire of a neighboring section.

Now, finally, the end was in sight. By the beginning of November the famed Hindenburg Line had been broken and the enemy was in retreat along the front. They were able to stop and put up fierce resistance at times, but they were short of men and supplies and could not continue to face the unrelenting attacks of the Allies.

In the early days of November the weather was extremely bad and operational patrols were severely limited by both sides. However, on November 10 Major Maxwell Kirby of the American First Pursuit Group scored his first and only victory. This was also the last Allied air victory of the war.

Facts and Figures

Chapter Fifteen

WHEN THE GREAT NATIONS sat down after the war and compiled their statistics, the figures were appalling. During those four years the wealth of the world had been turned into guns and grenades, bullets and tanks, battleships and submarines, poison gas and airplanes. More money had been spent for death and destruction than anyone could have dreamed possible.

But the money was of no consequence in comparison with the dreadful number of men who had been sacrificed. The total number killed and wounded was more than 29,757,700. Of these, some 17,983,000 had been members of the Allied forces, while Germany and the remaining Central Powers suffered approximately 11,775,000 casualties.

During this carnage the airplane had grown up—but the price for such progress had been prohibitive. When the guns first started firing the airplane was virtually a helpless infant; four years later it had developed into a reliable vehicle to transport men with reasonable safety at speeds which the Wright brothers in December 1903 could not have dreamed possible. In just fifteen short years, a miracle of progress had been wrought, and most of it had been brought about by the war.

It is difficult to wade through the statistics and come up with a truly accurate picture of the state of aviation among the belligerent powers at the end of the war. The official records indicate that at the Armistice the British Royal Air Force was composed of 22,647 aircraft of all types. However, this impressive figure dwindles to a mere 4,429 in operational status on the fighting fronts, with another 336 assigned to home defense. Of the 4,429 front-line machines, 1,799 were in France while the remaining 2,630 were scattered on other fronts from Italy to Macedonia. In addition to these, there were also approximately 180 aircraft attached to the Independent Air Force.

Despite the confusion of figures, there is no doubt that aviation had developed to a startling degree in England during those years. At the beginning of hostilities British aircraft were the worst possible examples of trial-and-error. Because of the almost complete lack of aeronautical knowledge and manufacturing facilities, the budding Royal Flying Corps was forced to depend to a great extent upon the French to build the airplanes for its squadrons. At the final count, more than 40,000 machines had been rolled from the production lines, among them some of the finest examples of aeronautical engineering that had ever taken wing.

The French originated the "ace" system, but this was never recognized by the British. The British thought of their airmen not as an elite corps but merely part of a gigantic fighting team. Even when Albert Ball was killed, the official thinking was that while his death was tragic, it was no more tragic than the death of an unglorified infantryman in the trenches.

When the Armistice came the French were probably more relieved than any of the other Allies. Not only had an entire generation of her young men been sacrificed in battle but the fighting had destroyed great sections of the country. French production had also been burdened to capacity, turning out some 51,000 airplanes for her own forces, the British, Belgians, Russians, and Americans. At the end, 12,919 officers and men were in flying service with the *escadrilles*.

The French, like the British, insisted upon concrete confirmation before victories were credited to pilots. Gilbert Sardier, for example, claimed his fifteenth victory on October 15, 1918, but did not receive confirmation until the wreckage of his victim was located after the Armistice. Against this, some of the more celebrated aces submitted claims for victories that had not been witnessed by observers, and these were not doubted.

The criteria for crediting victories was as rigid in the German Air Force as it was in the British and French, but here again no truly accurate picture can be drawn. Total German claims amounted to 7,577 aircraft and 552 balloons, while it is known that the actual figure was much higher. At the same time, a few of the aces were not questioned. Even with this laxity in some cases, Manfred von Richthofen was never given credit for the two victories he claimed prior to joining Oswald Boelcke's *Jasta* 2, even though one of these was mentioned in a communiqué from the front.

During the course of the war the Germans produced a total of 48,537 aircraft, which was just slightly more than half the total British and French production. On November 11, 1918, the German Air Force consisted of about 15,000 aircraft of all types, 4,050 of which were in operational units.

Statistically, the aerial records of the United States are the most confusing of all, even though American airmen were in combat only about seven months. Following the war General William Mitchell wrote: "My figures show that from the time that American air units entered into combat on the front . . . our men shot down and received official confirmation for 927 enemy airplanes or balloons. During the same time we lost, due to operations of the enemy, 316 of our airplanes or balloons." Official U.S. Air Service figures disagree with these totals, claiming 854 German aircraft and balloons against a loss of 337 aircraft and balloons.

At least part of this discrepancy must be attributed to the American recording system, which was considerably different from those of the other warring powers. On February 9, 1920,

Captain Edward Rickenbacker with his Spad S-13. While Rickenbacker scored most of his victories with a Spad, he preferred the
earlier Nieuport.   *U.S. Air Force*

the Director of the U.S. Air Service issued an official listing of all American airmen who were credited with confirmed victories, though with the following explanation:

> An addition of the victories listed herein does not furnish the number of enemy aircraft destroyed, due to the fact that the Air Service method of crediting gave each person who participated in combat one victory. Thus, if three were concerned in one fight to the destruction of one enemy airplane each United States combatant would be credited with one victory, if properly confirmed, but the enemy loss would still be but one airplane.

The number of airmen on this official list is 544, and their confirmed victories add up to 1,466. Captain Rickenbacker is also listed as having scored twenty-five victories rather than the twenty-six usually attributed to him.

But while the record of combat victories and losses by the United States is confusing, there was nothing confusing about the way American pilots faced their duty. When Congress declared war on Germany on April 6, 1917, the country's military air arm was in deplorable condition. By the time of the Armistice, America had fielded forty-five squadrons with 740 airplanes, 767 pilots, and 481 observers. Total Air Service complement at that time was 7,738 pilots and 70,769 enlisted men.

Air Service pilots flew more than 35,000 hours over enemy lines. In all, they made almost 13,000 fighter flights, approximately 6,600 observation flights, and more than 1,100 bombing missions. Total weight of bombs dropped was 112.5 tons.

Aircraft production in the United States became such a national scandal that the air industry was investigated. Following this investigation, Supreme Court Justice Charles Evans Hughes condemned the industry in a blistering indictment and said he regretted that "the provisions of the criminal statutes do not reach inefficiency." In fairness, however, the country as a whole, including Congress, should have borne considerable blame. The first practical airplane had been built in the United States, yet aeronautical development was neglected shamefully while the rest of the world forged ahead. Knowledge, more than money, was required to build an air force, and that knowledge had been denied American manufacturers by lack of official interest as well as lack of production orders.

As an example of the pathetic condition of American equipment, in October 1918 the newly formed 155th Aero Squadron was equipped with obsolete British F.E.2b's—a type that the Royal Flying Corps had withdrawn from day-fighter operations about a year and a half earlier.

Between July 1917 and the Armistice, the U.S. Air Service accepted 11,754 airplanes of all types from American and Canadian builders. Of these, only 1,213 D.H.4's actually reached France, and not one was truly fit for combat operations. After the initial period of growth had been passed some truly excellent home-designed aircraft had been built and tested. If the war had continued, these machines would probably have erased the first stigma of manufacturing inefficiency.

Following the war, when most of the wounds and hatreds had been healed or washed away, many tributes were written to the men who had fought and died in the skies. One of the least biased of these was by a German statesman named Otto Gessler. He said in part:

> History will provide few examples of greater courageous self-sacrifice than that written into the annals of the World War by the daring spirits of all sides who followed their duties and found their fate in the air. They fought in an element new to war; they accepted and braved dangers unknown before; they were the young, the quick, and the keen of all who fought, and admiration for their deeds is non-partisan.

The wreckage of a German airplane in a French field. Thousands of courageous airmen on both sides had died in the war, but finally it was over.   *U.S. Air Force*

American Aces with the A.E.F.

Score	Rank and Name	Score	Rank and Name
26	Captain Edward V. Rickenbacker	7	First Lieutenant Leslie J. Rummel
21	Second Lieutenant Frank Luke Jr.	7	First Lieutenant Karl J. Schoen
17	Major Raoul Lufbery	7	Captain Sumner Sewell
13	First Lieutenant George A. Vaughn Jr.	7	First Lieutenant William H. Stovall
12	Captain Field E. Kindley	6	First Lieutenant Byrne V. Baucom
12	First Lieutenant David E. Putnam	6	First Lieutenant James D. Beane
12	Captain Elliott W. Springs	6	Captain Arthur R. Brooks
10	Major Reed G. Landis	6	Captain Douglas Campbell
10	Captain Jacques M. Swaab	6	Captain Edward P. Curtis
9	First Lieutenant Lloyd A. Hamilton	6	First Lieutenant Murray K. Guthrie
9	Captain Frank O. Hunter	6	Captain James N. Hall
9	First Lieutenant Chester E. Wright	6	Captain Leonard C. Hammond
8	First Lieutenant Paul F. Baer	6	Lieutenant Colonel Harold E. Hartney
8	Major Charles J. Biddle	6	First Lieutenant Frank K. Hayes
8	Captain Thomas G. Cassady	6	Captain Donald Hudson
8	First Lieutenant Henry R. Clay Jr.	6	Major James A. Keating
8	Captain Hamilton Coolidge	6	Second Lieutenant Howard C. Knotts
8	First Lieutenant Jesse O. Creech	6	First Lieutenant Robert O. Lindsay
8	First Lieutenant William P. Erwin	6	First Lieutenant Ralph A. O'Neill
8	Second Lieutenant Clinton Jones	6	Major D. Peterson
8	Captain Gorman de F. Larner	6	First Lieutenant William T. Ponder
8	Major James A. Meissner	6	Second Lieutenant Kenneth L. Porter
8	First Lieutenant Joseph F. Wehner	6	Captain Martinus Stenseth
8	First Lieutenant Wilbur W. White Jr.	6	Lieutenant Colonel William K. Thaw
7	First Lieutenant Howard Burdick	6	Captain Edgar G. Tobin
7	Major Reed McK. Chambers	6	Captain Jerry C. Vasconelles
7	First Lieutenant Harvey W. Cook	5	First Lieutenant William T. Badham
7	First Lieutenant Lansing C. Holden	5	First Lieutenant Hilbert L. Bair
7	Major John W. Huffer	5	Captain Clayton L. Bissell
7	First Lieutenant John K. McArthur	5	Captain Harold R. Buckley
7	First Lieutenant Wendel A. Robertson	5	First Lieutenant Lawrence K. Calahan

Score	Rank and Name
5	Captain Everett R. Cook
5	First Lieutenant Arthur E. Easterbrook
5	First Lieutenant H. Clay Ferguson
5	First Lieutenant George W. Furlow
5	First Lieutenant Harold H. George
5	Captain Charles G. Gray
5	First Lieutenant Edward M. Haight
5	Captain James A. Healy
5	Lieutenant David S. Ingalls
5	First Lieutenant James Knowles Jr.
5	First Lieutenant Frederick E. Luff
5	Second Lieutenant J. Sidney Owens
5	First Lieutenant Orville A. Ralston
5	First Lieutenant John J. Seerley
5	Major Victor H. Strahm
5	First Lieutenant Francis M. Symonds
5	Captain William D. Tipton
5	Second Lieutenant Robert M. Todd
5	First Lieutenant Remington De B. Vernam
5	First Lieutenant Rodney D. Williams

AMERICAN ACES WITH THE FRENCH AIR SERVICE

Score	Rank and Name
12	Second Lieutenant Frank L. Baylies
8	Lieutenant James J. Connelly
8	Lieutenant Edwin C. Parsons
5	Lieutenant Ewart S. Miller
5	Lieutenant Norman Prince
5	Lieutenant Charles H. Veil

AMERICAN ACES WITH THE ROYAL AIR FORCE

Score	Rank and Name
23	Captain S. W. Rosevear
20	Flight Sub-Lieutenant J. J. Malone
19	Major A. M. Wilkinson
18	Captain F. L. Hale
18	Captain A. T. Iaccaci
16	Captain W. Gillette
15	Lieutenant C. T. Warman
14	Captain F. Libby
11	Lieutenant P. T. Iaccaci
10	Lieutenant L. L. Richardson
9	Captain O. J. Rose
8	Captain J. O. Donaldson
8	Lieutenant D. I. Lamb
7	Major F. I. Lord
6	Lieutenant F. A. Robertson
5	Lieutenant A. Matthews
5	Captain W. J. Pace
5	Lieutenant F. Westing

Belgian Aces

Score	Rank and Name	Score	Rank and Name
37	Captain Willy Coppens	7	Captain Fernand Jacquet
11	Adjutant André de Meulemeester	6	Lieutenant Jan Olieslagers
10	Second Lieutenant Edmond Thieffry		

British Aces

Score	Rank and Name	Score	Rank and Name
73	Major Edward Mannock	23	Captain D. Latimer
72	Lieutenant Colonel William A. Bishop	23	Captain E. J. McLoughry
		23	Lieutenant A. P. Rhys Davids
60	Lieutenant Colonel Raymond Collishaw	23	Captain H. A. Whistler
		22	Major C. D. Booker
57	Major James T. McCudden	22	Major W. J. Cochrane-Patrick
54	Captain Anthony W. Beauchamp-Proctor	22	Captain R. King
		22	Lieutenant McK. Thomson
54	Major Donald R. MacLaren	22	Captain C. J. Venter
53	Major William G. Barker	21	Captain P. J. Clayson
47	Captain Robert A. Little	21	Captain R. P. Minifie
46	Captain Philip F. Fullard	21	Captain G. E. Thompson
46	Captain George E. McElroy	20	Captain D. J. Bell
44	Captain Albert Ball	20	Captain T. S. Harrison
44	Captain John Gilmore	20	Captain W. L. Harrison
41	Major Tom F. Hazell	20	Captain E. C. Johnston
40	Captain J. Ira Jones	20	Captain C. F. King
39	Captain William G. Claxton	20	Captain I. D. McDonald
39	Major Roderic S. Dallas	20	Lieutenant C. M. MacEwen
37	Captain Frederick R. McCall	20	Major G. W. Murlis-Green
35	Captain Henry W. Woollett	20	Major K. R. Park
34	Captain Francis G. Quigley	20	Captain D. A. Stewart
32	Major Geoffrey H. Bowman	19	Captain W. Beaver
31	Major Albert D. Carter	19	Captain H. B. Bell-Irving
31	Captain J. L. White	19	Captain W. MacLanachan
30	Captain M. B. Frew	19	Major S. M. Miles
30	Captain S. M. Kinkead	19	Captain H. W. Saunders
30	Captain A. E. McKeever	18	Lieutenant L. M. Barlow
29	Captain A. H. Cobby	18	Lieutenant C. F. Collett
29	Captain W. L. Jordon	18	Captain A. K. Cowper
27	Captain J. E. Gurdon	18	Captain F. R. Cubbon
27	Captain R. T. Hoidge	18	Captain E. Dickson
27	Captain H. G. Luchford	18	Captain A. J. Enstone
27	Major G. J. Maxwell	18	Lieutenant E. V. Reid
26	Captain W. C. Campbell	18	Captain F. A. Thayre
26	Captain W. E. Staton	18	Captain J. L. Trollope
25	Major K. L. Caldwell	18	Lieutenant W. B. Wood
25	Major R. J. Compston	17	Captain J. H. Burden
25	Major J. Leacroft	17	Captain G. H. Cock
25	Captain R. A. Mayberry	17	Captain L. F. Jenkins
24	Major J. O. Andrews	17	Captain M. A. Nounhouse
24	Captain W. E. Shields	17	Captain Edwin Swale
23	Captain J. S. Fall	16	Captain O. M. Baldwin
23	Captain A. Hepburn	16	Captain C. R. Hickey

Score	Rank and Name	Score	Rank and Name
16	Captain H. T. Mellings	12	Captain N. W. Webb
16	Captain T. P. Middleton	12	Major J. T. Whittaker
16	Lieutenant S. A. Oades	12	Captain P. Wilson
16	Major K. Oxspring	11	Captain S. Carlin
16	Major S. F. Pender	11	Captain R. E. Dodds
16	Captain B. Roxburgh-Smith	11	Captain G. B. Gates
15	Captain P. C. Carpenter	11	Captain H. A. Hamersley
15	Captain M. H. Findley	11	Captain S. C. Joseph
15	Captain R. A. Grosvenor	11	Captain A. C. Kiddie
15	Lieutenant H. B. Richardson	11	Captain K. M. Leaske
15	Captain J. H. Tudhope	11	Captain C. N. Lowe
15	Captain W. A. Tyrell	11	Lieutenant A. McCudden
14	Captain M. Galbraith	11	Lieutenant R. W. McKenzie
14	Captain G. E. Gibbs	11	Captain N. McMillan
14	Captain S. W. Highwood	11	Lieutenant A. J. Morgan
14	Major N. F. McEwan	11	Captain W. R. Pearson
14	Captain R. T. Mark	11	Lieutenant A. E. Reed
13	Captain C. P. Brown	11	Captain W. W. Rogers
13	Captain R. A. Delhaye	11	Captain M. D. Scott
13	Captain J. H. Hedley	11	Lieutenant J. E. Sharman
13	Captain A. G. Jones-Williams	11	Captain S. F. Thompson
13	Lieutenant C. H. Lagesse	10	Major B. E. Baker
13	Lieutenant N. W. Mawle	10	Captain G. B. Baker
13	Captain G. P. Olley	10	Captain C. C. Banks
13	Captain H. G. Reeves	10	Captain J. A. Boswell
13	Captain C. G. Ross	10	Lieutenant G. L. Graham
13	Lieutenant Colonel A. J. Scott	10	Captain E. T. Hayne
13	Captain F. R. Smith	10	Lieutenant T. S. Horry
13	Captain O. H. Vickers	10	Captain W. H. Hubbard
12	Lieutenant L. B. Bennit	10	Captain V. Kearley
12	Captain A. R. Brown	10	Captain D. V. MacGregor
12	Captain R. W. Chappell	10	Lieutenant R. M. Makepeace
12	Captain E. S. Coler	10	Lieutenant R. F. Maudit
12	Captain C. M. Crowe	10	Captain J. W. Pinder
12	Major C. Draper	10	Lieutenant H. B. Redler
12	Captain H. F. Drewitt	10	Lieutenant T. Rose
12	Lieutenant Alan Gerrard	10	Captain J. Scott
12	Lieutenant F. D. Gillete	10	Captain S. P. Smith
12	Major P. Huskinson	10	Captain A. T. Tonks
12	Captain H. P. Lale	10	Lieutenant K. R. Unger
12	Lieutenant M. E. Mealing	10	Major G. M. Vaucour
12	Lieutenant K. B. Montgomery	10	Lieutenant H. G. Watson
12	Lieutenant Colonel R. H. Mulock	10	Lieutenant W. L. Wells
12	Major R. C. Phillips	10	Major W. E. Young
12	Captain L. H. Rochford	9	Lieutenant C. G. Boothroyd
12	Captain W. A. Southey	9	Captain D. C. Cunnell
12	Lieutenant L. T. Taplin	9	Lieutenant H. Edwards
12	Lieutenant F. D. Travers	9	Captain J. C. Firth

Score	Rank and Name	Score	Rank and Name
9	Captain J. Fitzmaurice	8	Lieutenant P. A. McDougall
9	Lieutenant T. M. Harries	8	Lieutenant J. A. Mann
9	Major L. G. Hawker	8	Captain R. L. Manuel
9	Lieutenant J. A. Hone	8	Lieutenant A. Mussared
9	Lieutenant W. R. Irwin	8	Lieutenant J. E. Nash
9	Captain M. R. James	8	Lieutenant E. C. Pashley
9	Sergeant F. Johnson	8	Lieutenant C. W. Payton
9	Lieutenant E. G. Lussier	8	Lieutenant L. F. Powell
9	Captain F. McQuistan	8	Lieutenant A. F. Pritchard
9	Captain W. E. Mann	8	Lieutenant C. R. Richards
9	Captain R. Manzer	8	Lieutenant A. S. Shepherd
9	Lieutenant J. F. Mellersh	8	Lieutenant J. W. Warner
9	Captain M. R. Ross Smith	8	Captain J. B. White
9	Second Lieutenant I. L. Roy	8	Lieutenant A. M. Wilkinson
9	Lieutenant W. Sidebottom	7	Captain J. W. Aldred
9	Lieutenant G. Thomson	7	Captain W. M. Alexander
9	Captain J. Todd	7	Captain A. C. Atkey
9	Captain R. M. Trevethan	7	Corporal A. Beebee
9	Lieutenant H. L. Waddington	7	Captain T. H. Blaxland
8	Lieutenant C. N. Armison	7	Captain W. A. Bond
8	Captain E. D. Atkinson	7	Captain A. J. Bott
8	Captain T. C. Baker	7	Captain R. C. Brading
8	Captain E. B. Betts	7	Captain C. A. Brewster-Joske
8	Lieutenant B. S. Breadner	7	Captain E. W. Broadberry
8	Lieutenant W. H. Brown	7	Captain O. C. Bryson
8	Lieutenant G. W. Bulmer	7	Lieutenant A. Buchanan
8	Captain H. Daniel	7	Captain R. M. Charley
8	Lieutenant H. Dolan	7	Lieutenant E. A. Clear
8	Captain A. Dover-Atkinson	7	Captain A. C. Cole
8	Captain T. Durrant	7	Captain J. Cottle
8	Captain J. H. Forman	7	Lieutenant E. A. Daly
8	Captain C. V. Gardiner	7	Lieutenant C. H. Dickins
8	Captain G. E. Gibbons	7	Captain G. Duncan
8	Captain F. Godfrey	7	Lieutenant W. Durrand
8	Captain H. K. Goode	7	Captain C. Farrell
8	Lieutenant R. Gordon	7	Captain W. H. Farrow
8	Lieutenant J. S. Griffith	7	Captain W. S. Fielding-Johnson
8	Captain J. D. Harman	7	Lieutenant R. M. Fletcher
8	Captain W. F. Harvey	7	Captain H. G. Forrest
8	Captain A. S. Hemming	7	Major T. F. Gerrard
8	Captain O. A. Heron	7	Captain C. B. Glynn
8	Major F. Holliday	7	Major S. J. Goble
8	Lieutenant D. C. Inglis	7	Captain W. B. Green
8	Lieutenant W. S. Jenkins	7	Captain H. J. Hamilton
8	Lieutenant K. W. Junor	7	Lieutenant F. J. Hunt
8	Captain N. Keeble	7	Lieutenant A. Jenks
8	Captain P. A. Langan-Byrne	7	Lieutenant L. B. Jones
8	Captain C. A. Lewis	7	Lieutenant E. P. Kennedy

Score	Rank and Name	Score	Rank and Name
7	Major S. H. Long	6	Captain S. E. Cowan
7	Lieutenant W. M. MacDonald	6	Captain C. W. Cudemore
7	Captain M. C. McGregor	6	Lieutenant J. J. Dawe
7	Captain C. M. Maud	6	Captain R. J. Dawes
7	Captain W. R. May	6	Sergeant E. J. Elton
7	Captain H. M. Moody	6	Captain D. L. Evans
7	Captain G. B. Moore	6	Captain A. B. Fairclough
7	Major R. B. Munday	6	Lieutenant A. L. Fleming
7	Major A. Murray-Jones	6	Captain G. B. Foster
7	Captain I. P. Napier	6	Lieutenant R. W. Fumer
7	Captain J. D. Payne	6	Captain F. J. Gibbs
7	Lieutenant C. R. Pithy	6	Sergeant Mechanic J. Grant
7	Lieutenant Colonel C. F. Portal	6	Captain R. Gregory
7	Captain A. C. Randall	6	Captain D. Grinnell-Milne
7	Major R. Raymond-Barker	6	Captain E. D. Gundall
7	Captain O. W. Redgate	6	Lieutenant A. J. Haines
7	Captain J. M. Robb	6	Lieutenant L. Hamilton
7	Lieutenant E. M. Roberts	6	Lieutenant G. S. Haymard
7	Captain R. H. Rusby	6	Captain H. G. Hegarty
7	Captain H. L. Satchell	6	Lieutenant E. D. Hicks
7	Captain C. R. Steele	6	Captain W. C. Hilburn
7	Lieutenant C. O. Stones	6	Lieutenant D'A. F. Hilton
7	Major W. V. Strugnall	6	Captain S. B. Horn
7	Captain S. T. Todd	6	Lieutenant H. B. Hudson
7	Captain H. E. Walker	6	Captain G. Irving
7	Lieutenant H. S. Walkerdine	6	Captain G. R. Jones
7	Captain S. H. Wallage	6	Captain N. C. Jones
7	Captain H. L. Wallis	6	Gun-Layer W. Jones
7	Lieutenant F. C. Wilton	6	Lieutenant G. S. Jones-Evans
7	Captain J. W. Woodhouse	6	Lieutenant H. A. Kolbury
6	Lieutenant G. F. Apps	6	Captain J. H. Letts
6	Lieutenant L. A. Ashfield	6	Lieutenant T. A. Lewis
6	Lieutenant G. G. Bailey	6	Captain C. McEvoy
6	Sergeant J. M. Bainbridge	6	Flight Lieutenant C. R. MacKenzie
6	Captain R. B. Bannerman	6	Captain R. G. Malcolm
6	Captain F. L. Barwell	6	Captain G. F. Malley
6	Captain J. D. Belgrave	6	Lieutenant D. J. Moore
6	Captain H. B. Bell	6	Captain E. T. Morrow
6	Lieutenant G. A. Birks	6	Lieutenant K. K. Muspratt
6	Captain H. A. Biziou	6	Captain G. C. Napier
6	Captain W. O. Boger	6	Sergeant A. Newland
6	Major C. J. Brand	6	Lieutenant A. J. Palliser
6	Captain H. Brooks	6	Captain A. A. Pentland
6	Captain F. E. Brown	6	Captain C. F. Pineau
6	Captain R. J. Brownell	6	Captain T. L. Purdom
6	Captain P. S. Burge	6	Captain J. S. Ralston
6	Captain D. H. de Burgh	6	Captain F. C. Ransley
6	Captain W. J. Cairns		

Score	Rank and Name	Score	Rank and Name
6	Lieutenant H. C. Rath	5	Lieutenant H. G. Crowe
6	Lieutenant H. R. Rhodes	5	Captain G. L. Cruikshank
6	Captain H. S. Saint	5	Captain E. D. Cummings
6	Lieutenant T. Seaman-Green	5	Captain W. A. Curtis
6	Captain W. Selwyn	5	Captain S. Dalrymple
6	Lieutenant R. H. Sloley	5	Lieutenant E. C. Davies
6	Captain R. R. Soar	5	Captain F. J. Davies
6	Captain S. Stanger	5	Captain G. C. Dixon
6	Captain W. S. Stephenson	5	Captain W. A. Duncan
6	Major O. Stewart	5	Lieutenant R. Dunston
6	Captain B. Strange	5	Captain S. T. Edwards
6	Major R. N. Stuart-Wortley	5	Captain W. R. Fish
6	Captain O. M. Sutton	5	Captain R. M. Foster
6	Lieutenant F. S. Symondson	5	Captain M. M. Freehill
6	Lieutenant C. R. Thompson	5	Captain W. M. Fry
6	Lieutenant R. W. Turner	5	Lieutenant J. V. Gascoyne
6	Captain A. W. Vigers	5	Lieutenant G. W. Gauld
6	Lieutenant F. G. Weare	5	Lieutenant H. R. Gauld
6	Lieutenant D. J. Weston	5	Lieutenant W. B. Giles
6	Lieutenant R. Winnicott	5	Lieutenant C. G. Glass
6	Captain A. B. Yuille	5	Captain A. S. Godfrey
5	Captain L. W. Allen	5	Captain M. E. Gonne
5	Lieutenant E. O. Amm	5	Lieutenant F. R. Gordon
5	Major H. H. Balfour	5	Lieutenant J. R. Gordon
5	Captain H. F. Beamish	5	Captain E. R. Grange
5	Captain A. Beck	5	Captain J. E. Hallonquist
5	Lieutenant E. L. Benhow	5	Captain R. G. Hammersley
5	Captain M. A. Benjamin	5	Captain I. H. Henderson
5	Captain G. N. Blennerhassett	5	Captain R. G. Hewitt
5	Captain G. H. Boarman	5	Lieutenant L. N. Hollinghurst
5	Lieutenant R. Bollinds	5	Captain O. Horsley
5	Lieutenant S. McG. Brown	5	Lieutenant G. R. Howsam
5	Captain D. H. Carberry	5	Captain E. C. Hoy
5	Captain W. M. Carlaw	5	Sergeant E. C. Hunt
5	Lieutenant R. N. Chandler	5	Captain J. E. Hunter
5	Captain J. S. Chick	5	Captain L. W. Jarvis
5	Lieutenant E. D. Clark	5	Lieutenant E. R. Jeffree
5	Lieutenant H. G. Clements	5	Lieutenant C. H. Jeffs
5	Captain C. Cockerall	5	Captain O. C. Johnsen
5	Captain D. G. Cooke	5	Captain A. G. Knight
5	Captain L. P. Coombes	5	Captain E. E. Kingsford-Smith
5	Lieutenant H. A. Cooper	5	Captain F. H. Laurence
5	Captain N. Cooper	5	Lieutenant G. E. Lawson
5	Lieutenant E. F. Crabbe	5	Lieutenant E. W. Lindeberg
5	Second Lieutenant W. B. Craig	5	Captain G. L. Lloyd
5	Captain K. Crawford	5	Captain W. H. Longton
5	Lieutenant K. Crossen	5	Lieutenant G. Luff
5	Lieutenant R. C. Crowden	5	Lieutenant R. K. McConnell

Score	Rank and Name	Score	Rank and Name
5	Captain A. McGregor	5	Captain F. H. Selous
5	Lieutenant E. A. McKay	5	Captain T. S. Sharpe
5	Captain J. H. McNearney	5	Major W. Sholto-Douglas
5	Lieutenant F. P. Magoun	5	Captain F. O. Soden
5	Lieutenant W. D. Matheson	5	Lieutenant A. R. Spurling
5	Lieutenant W. G. Meggitt	5	Sergeant T. F. Stephenson
5	Lieutenant F. T. Menendez	5	Captain F. D. Stevens
5	Captain J. Mitchell	5	Captain V. R. Stoakes
5	Captain W. E. Molesworth	5	Captain M. Thomas
5	Captain H. A. Molyneux	5	Lieutenant W. M. Thomson
5	Lieutenant J. L. Morgan	5	Captain D. M. Tidmarsh
5	Lieutenant L. L. Morgan	5	Lieutenant N. C. Trescowthick
5	Captain H. A. Patey	5	Second Lieutenant J. H. Umney
5	Lieutenant D. S. Poller	5	Lieutenant E. R. Varley
5	Captain G. W. Price	5	Lieutenant R. B. Wainwright
5	Captain P. B. Prothero	5	Captain A. G. Waller
5	Major G. R. Reid	5	Captain G. W. Wareing
5	Captain A. Rice-Oxley	5	Captain A. T. Whealey
5	Lieutenant N. Roberts	5	Captain F. T. Williams
5	Lieutenant A. E. Robertson	5	Captain T. M. Williams
5	Major H. A. van Ryneveld	5	Lieutenant C. M. Wilson
5	Lieutenant Colonel W. D. Sanday	5	Major H. A. Wood
5	Captain F. G. Saunders	5	Lieutenant A. E. Woodbridge
5	Captain O. J. Scholte		

French Aces

Score	Rank and Name	Score	Rank and Name
75	Captain René Fonck	11	Sub-Lieutenant Léon Nuville
54	Captain Georges Guynemer	11	Lieutenant Jacques Ortoli
45	Lieutenant Charles Nungesser	10	Adjutant Maurice Bizot
41	Captain Georges Madon	10	Adjutant André Chainat
35	Sub-Lieutenant Maurice Boyeau	10	Adjutant Marcel Gasser
34	Sub-Lieutenant Michel Coiffard	10	Sub-Lieutenant André Herbelin
28	Sub-Lieutenant Jean Bourjade	10	Captain Auguste Lahoulle
27	Captain Armand Pinsard	10	Adjutant Charles Macé
23	Sub-Lieutenant René Dorme	10	Adjutant Jean Pezon
23	Lieutenant Gabriel Guérin	10	Sub-Lieutenant Charles Quette
23	Sub-Lieutenant Claude Haegelen	10	Sub-Lieutenant Robert Waddington
22	Sub-Lieutenant Pierre Marinovitch	9	Captain Fernand Bonneton
21	Captain Alfred Heurtaux	9	Sub-Lieutenant Marcel Coadou
20	Captain Albert Deullin	9	Sub-Lieutenant Henri Condemine
19	Captain Henri de Slade	9	Sub-Lieutenant Gilbert de Guingand
19	Lieutenant Jacques Ehrlich	9	Captain Mathieu de la Tour
18	Lieutenant Bernard de Romanet	9	Sub-Lieutenant Marcel Dorme
16	Lieutenant Jean Chaput	9	Adjutant Gustave Douchy
15	Captain Paul d'Argueeff	9	Sub-Lieutenant René Dousinelle
15	Captain Armand de Turenne	9	Lieutenant André Gros
15	Lieutenant Gilbert Sardier	9	Captain Georges Matton
14	Sub-Lieutenant Marc Ambrogi	9	Sub-Lieutenant Marcel Viallet
13	Sub-Lieutenant Omer Demeuldre	8	Sub-Lieutenant Paul Barbreau
13	Lieutenant Hector Garaud	8	Adjutant Fernand Chauvannes
13	Lieutenant Marcel Noguès	8	Sub-Lieutenant Dieudonné Costes
12	Sub-Lieutenant Bernard Artigau	8	Sub-Lieutenant André de Cordoux
12	Lieutenant Jean Casale	8	Major Robert de Marancour
12	Sub-Lieutenant Gustave Daladier	8	Captain Jacques Gérard
12	Captain Xavier de Sévin	8	Adjutant Antoine Laplasse
12	Sub-Lieutenant Fernand Guyou	8	Adjutant Edmond Pillon
12	Lieutenant Marcel Hugues	8	Captain Roger Poupon
12	Sub-Lieutenant Lucien Jailler	8	Sergeant Paul Sauvage
12	Captain Jacques Leps	8	Sub-Lieutenant Gaston Vial
12	Sub-Lieutenant Jean Navarre	7	Captain Alfred Auger
12	Lieutenant Paul Tarascon	7	Sergeant André Bosson
11	Adjutant Armand Berthelot	7	Sub-Lieutenant Roger Bretillon
11	Sub-Lieutenant Jean Bouyer	7	Lieutenant Carl de Kerlande
11	Lieutenant Benjamen Bozon-Verduraz	7	Adjutant François Delzenne
11	Sub-Lieutenant William Hérisson	7	Captain René Doumer
11	Adjutant Maxime Lenoir	7	Captain Raoul Echard
11	Sub-Lieutenant Ernest Maunoury		
11	Adjutant René Montrion		

Score	Rank and Name	Score	Rank and Name
7	Sub-Lieutenant Georges Flachaire	6	Sergeant Constant Soulier
7	Captain Georges Lachmann	5	Sub-Lieutenant Barbaza
7	Lieutenant Henry Languedoc	5	Adjutant Marcel Bloch
7	Lieutenant Jean Loste	5	Lieutenant Georges Boillot
7	Lieutenant Alex Marty	5	Adjutant Alexandre Buisson
7	Sergeant Jean Moissinac	5	Adjutant Calliau
7	Lieutenant Pierre Pendaris	5	Lieutenant Lucien Cayol
7	Adjutant Henri Peronneau	5	Lieutenant Robert Cordonnier
7	Adjutant Paul Petit	5	Lieutenant P. Leroy de Boiseaumarie
7	Sergeant Paul Santelle	5	Lieutenant Deboigne
7	Adjutant Victor Sayaret	5	Lieutenant Leon Debonald
7	Sub-Lieutenant Gabriel Thomas	5	Adjutant André Degennes
7	Adjutant Marie Vitalis	5	Lieutenant Jean-Paul de Tierrens
7	Major Joseph Vuillemin	5	Lieutenant V. G. Fedorov
6	Lieutenant François Battesti	5	Lieutenant Roland Garros
6	Lieutenant Alexandre Borzecki	5	Lieutenant Pierre Gaudermen
6	Sergeant Camplan	5	Lieutenant Julien Guertiau
6	Lieutenant Albert Chabrier	5	Sergeant Joseph Guiguet
6	Lieutenant Louis Coudouret	5	Adjutant Hamot
6	Sub-Lieutenant Jules Covin	5	Sub-Lieutenant Marius Hasdenteufel
6	Lieutenant Robert de Bonnefoy	5	Sergeant Marcel Hauss
6	Sergeant Adolphe d'Aische	5	Adjutant Marcel Henroit
6	Adjutant Pierre Delage	5	Lieutenant Paul Homo
6	Lieutenant René Delannoy	5	Captain Didier Lecour-Grandmaison
6	Sub-Lieutenant André Delorme	5	Adjutant Georges Leinhart
6	Captain Jean Derode	5	Captain Paul Malavielle
6	Lieutenant Edmond de Gavardie	5	Private Louis Martin
6	Lieutenant de Marmier	5	Adjutant Naudin
6	Adjutant Pierre de Pralines	5	Adjutant André Petit-Delchet
6	Sub-Lieutenant H. Noel de Rochefort	5	Sub-Lieutenant Plessis
6	Sergeant André Dubonnet	5	Sub-Lieutenant Portron
6	Sub-Lieutenant Jean Fraissinet	5	Sub-Lieutenant Louis Risacher
6	Captain Paul Gastin	5	Adjutant Maurice Robert
6	Lieutenant Maurice Gond	5	Adjutant Maurice Rousselle
6	Captain Albert Mezergues	5	Captain Jean Sabatier
6	Sub-Lieutenant Adolphe Pégoud	5	Adjutant Paul Violet
6	Captain Georges Raymond	5	Lieutenant Pierre Wertheimer
6	Adjutant Victor Régnier		
6	Sergeant Achille Rousseau		

German Aces

Score	Rank and Name	Score	Rank and Name
80	Captain of Cavalry Manfred von Richthofen	27	Lieutenant Karl Thom
62	Lieutenant Colonel Ernst Udet	27	Captain Adolf von Tutschek
53	Lieutenant Colonel Erich Loewenhardt	27	Lieutenant Kurt Wüsthoff
48	Lieutenant Werner Voss	26	Lieutenant Colonel Harald Auffahrt
45	Lieutenant Fritz Rumey	26	Lieutenant Colonel Oscar von Boenigk
44	Captain Rudolf Berthold	26	Lieutenant Colonel Eduard Dostler
44	Captain Bruno Loerzer	26	Lieutenant Arthur Laumann
43	Lieutenant Paul Bäumer	25	Lieutenant Oliver von Beaulieu-Marconnay
41	Lieutenant Josef Jacobs	25	Lieutenant Colonel Robert von Greim
40	Captain Oswald Boelcke	25	Lieutenant Georg von Hantelmann
40	Lieutenant Franz Büchner	25	Lieutenant Max Näther
40	Lieutenant Colonel Lothar von Richthofen	25	Lieutenant Fritz Pütter
39	Lieutenant Heinrich Gontermann	24	Lieutenant Erwin Böhme
39	Lieutenant Karl Menckoff	23	Lieutenant Hermann Becker
36	Lieutenant Max Müller	23	Lieutenant Georg Meyer
35	Lieutenant Julius Buckler	22	Lieutenant Colonel Hermann Göring
35	Lieutenant Gustav Dörr	22	Lieutenant Hans Klein
35	Captain Eduard von Schleich	22	Lieutenant Hans Pippart
34	Lieutenant Josef Veltjens	22	Lieutenant Werner Preuss
33	Lieutenant Heinrich Bongartz	22	Sergeant Karl Schlegel
33	Lieutenant Otto Koennecke	22	Lieutenant Rudolf Windisch
33	Lieutenant Colonel Kurt Wolff	21	Lieutenant Hans Adam
32	Lieutenant Theo Osterkamp	21	Captain Friedrich Christiansen
32	Lieutenant Emil Thuy	21	Lieutenant Fritz Friedrichs
31	Lieutenant Paul Billik	21	Lieutenant Fritz Höhn
31	Captain of Cavalry Karl Bolle	20	Sergeant Friedrich Altemeier
31	Lieutenant Colonel Gotthard Sachenberg	20	Lieutenant Colonel Hans Bethge
30	Lieutenant Karl Allmenröder	20	Lieutenant Rudolf von Eschwege
30	Lieutenant Karl Degelow	20	Lieutenant Walter Goettsch
30	Lieutenant Heinrich Kroll	20	Lieutenant Friedrich Noltenius
30	Lieutenant Josef Mai	20	Captain Wilhelm Reinhard
30	Lieutenant Ulrich Neckel	19	Sergeant Gerhard Fieseler
30	Lieutenant Karl Schaefer	19	Lieutenant Wilhelm Frankl
29	Lieutenant Hermann Frommerz	19	Lieutenant Otto Kissenberth
28	Lieutenant Walter Blume	19	Lieutenant Colonel Otto Schmidt
28	Lieutenant Walter von Bülow	18	Lieutenant Hartmuth Baldamus
28	Lieutenant Colonel Fritz von Röth	18	Lieutenant Franz Hemer
27	Lieutenant Colonel Fritz Bernert	18	Sergeant Oscar Hennrich
27	Sergeant Otto Fruhner		
27	Lieutenant Hans Kirschstein		

Score	Rank and Name	Score	Rank and Name
18	Lieutenant Kurt Wintgens	12	Lieutenant Diether Collin
17	Lieutenant Walter Böning	12	Sergeant Gottfried Ehmann
17	Lieutenant Ernst Hess	12	Sergeant Otto Esswein
17	Lieutenant Franz Ray	12	Sergeant Sebastian Festner
17	Lieutenant Hans Rolfes	12	Lieutenant Walter Höhndorf
17	Sergeant Josef Schwendemann	12	Sergeant Man Kuhn
16	Lieutenant Hans Boehning	12	Sergeant Friedrich Manschott
16	Lieutenant Hans von Freden	12	Lieutenant Hans Mueller
16	Lieutenant Ludwig Hanstein	12	Lieutenant Colonel Franz Schleiff
16	Lieutenant Rudolf Klimke	12	Lieutenant Richard Wenzl
16	Lieutenant Karl Odebrett	11	Lieutenant Heinrich Arntzen
16	Lieutenant Hans Weiss	11	Lieutenant Raven von Barnekow
15	Sergeant Christian Donhauser	11	Lieutenant Joachim von Busse
15	Lieutenant Albert Dossenbach	11	Lieutenant Xaver Dannhuber
15	Sergeant Albert Haussmann	11	Lieutenant Colonel Kurt von Doering
15	Lieutenant Aloys Heldmann	11	Lieutenant Heinz Dreckmann
15	Lieutenant Colonel Max Immelmann	11	Sergeant Willi Gabriel
15	Lieutenant Johannes Klein	11	Lieutenant Hans von Keudell
15	Lieutenant Otto Löffler	11	Lieutenant Colonel Stephan Kirmaier
15	Lieutenant Victor von Pressentin	11	Lieutenant Alfred Lindenberger
15	Lieutenant Theodor Quandt	11	Lieutenant Fritz Loerzer
15	Lieutenant Julius Schmidt	11	Lieutenant Hermann Pfeiffer
15	Lieutenant Kurt Schneider	11	Lieutenant Hugo Schaefer
14	Lieutenant Ernst Bormann	11	Lieutenant Renatus Theiller
14	Sergeant Rudolf Francke	10	Corporal Paul Aue
14	Sergeant Edmund Nathanael	10	Sergeant Dietrich Averes
14	Lieutenant Franz Piechurek	10	Lieutenant Colonel Hans Berr
14	Lieutenant Karl Plauth	10	Lieutenant Franz Brandt
14	Sergeant Emil Schape	10	Sergeant Fritz Classen
14	Lieutenant Georg Schlenker	10	Lieutenant Martin Dehmisch
14	Sergeant Wilhelm Seitz	10	Lieutenant Wilhelm Frickart
14	Lieutenant Paul Straehle	10	Lieutenant Justus Grassman
14	Lieutenant Rudolf Wendelmuth	10	Lieutenant Rudolf Matthaei
13	Sergeant Karl Bohnenkamp	10	Lieutenant Max Mulzer
13	Lieutenant Joachim Büttner	10	Sergeant Alfons Nagler
13	Captain Hans Duddecke	10	Lieutenant Wilhelm Neuenhofen
13	Lieutenant Heinrich Geigl	10	Lieutenant Colonel Hans Schuez
13	Sergeant Robert Heibert	10	Lieutenant Werner Steinhäuser
13	Lieutenant Johann Janzen	10	Lieutenant Erich Thomas
13	Sergeant Reinhold Jörke	10	Lieutenant Paul Turck
13	Sergeant Christel Mesch	10	Sergeant Bernhard Ultsch
13	Sergeant Otto Rosenfeld	10	Lieutenant Paul Wenzel
13	Lieutenant Colonel Kurt Schoenfelder	10	Lieutenant Joachim Wolff
13	Lieutenant Colonel Rüdiger von Wedel	9	Lieutenant Colonel Ernst von Althaus
12	Lieutenant Colonel Theodor Cammann	9	Lieutenant Arno Benzler
		9	Lieutenant Otto Brauneck

Score	Rank and Name	Score	Rank and Name
9	Lieutenant Albert Dietlen	7	Lieutenant Karl Bohng
9	Lieutenant Otto Fitzner	7	Lieutenant Helmut Brünig
9	Lieutenant Karl Gallwitz	7	Lieutenant Otto Creutzmann
9	Sergeant Friedrich Huffzky	7	Lieutenant Helmut Diltheg
9	Lieutenant Herbert Knappe	7	Lieutenant Colonel Hans Gandert
9	Lieutenant Egon Koepsch	7	Lieutenant Herman Habich
9	Sergeant Fritz Kosmahl	7	Lieutenant Hans von Haebler
9	Lieutenant Walter Kypke	7	Captain Otto Hartmann
9	Lieutenant Gustav Leffers	7	Lieutenant Kurt Jacob
9	Lieutenant Paul Lotz	7	Lieutenant Martin Johns
9	Lieutenant Herbert Mahn	7	Sergeant Max Kahlow
9	Lieutenant Hans von der Marwitz	7	Lieutenant Franz Kirchfeld
9	Lieutenant Eberhardt Mohicke	7	Lieutenant Emil Koch
9	Lieutenant Hans Müller	7	Sergeant Wilhelm Kühne
9	Corporal Hans Nülle	7	Lieutenant Colonel Hans Kummetz
9	Sergeant Karl Pech	7	Lieutenant Helmut Lange
9	Sergeant Karl Schattauer	7	Lieutenant Hermann Leptien
9	Lieutenant Adolf Schulte	7	Sergeant Albert Lux
8	Lieutenant Leopold Anslinger	7	Lieutenant Heinrich Maushake
8	Lieutenant Aloys Brandenstein	7	Lieutenant Albert Mendel
8	Lieutenant Konrad Brendle	7	Lieutenant Kurt Monnington
8	Lieutenant Günther Dobberke	7	Lieutenant Alfred Niederhoff
8	Sergeant Friedrich Ehmann	7	Captain Henning von Osteroth
8	Lieutenant Colonel Walter Evers	7	Lieutenant Richard Plange
8	Lieutenant Max Gossner	7	Sergeant Johann Pütz
8	Lieutenant Wolfgang Güttler	7	Lieutenant Fritz Riemer
8	Sergeant Willi Hippert	7	Lieutenant Willi Rosenstein
8	Lieutenant Hans Hoyer	7	Sergeant Gustav Schneidewind
8	Corporal Paul Hüttenrauch	7	Sergeant Edgar Scholz
8	Sergeant Willi Kampe	7	Sergeant Georg Strasser
8	Lieutenant Fritz Kieckhaefer	7	Captain Franz Walz
8	Lieutenant Arthur Korff	7	Lieutenant Hans Werner
8	Lieutenant Otto Parschau	7	Corporal Wilhelm Zorn
8	Sergeant Friedrich Püschke	6	Sergeant Karl Arnold
8	Lieutenant Wolfram von Richthofen	6	Corporal Johann Baur
8	Lieutenant Karl Ritscherle	6	Sergeant Paul Bona
8	Lieutenant Richard Runge	6	Sergeant Adolf Borchers
8	Lieutenant Colonel Hans Schilling	6	Lieutenant Martin Bretschneider-Bodener
8	Lieutenant Viktor Schobinger	6	Lieutenant Harry von Bülow
8	Lieutenant Karl von Schonebeck	6	Lieutenant Colonel Hermann Dahlmann
8	Lieutenant Wilhelm Schwartz	6	Lieutenant Karl Deilman
8	Lieutenant Fritz Thiede	6	Lieutenant Julius Fichter
8	Lieutenant Georg Weiner	6	Lieutenant Gustav Frädrich
7	Lieutenant Gerhard Anders	6	Corporal Friedrich Gille
7	Lieutenant Gerhard Bassenge	6	Lieutenant Hermann Gilly
7	Lieutenant Ludwig Beckmann	6	Lieutenant Gisbert Groos

Score	Rank and Name	Score	Rank and Name
6	Lieutenant Colonel Fritz Grosch	5	Corporal Gustav Borm
6	Lieutenant Colonel Adolf Gutknecht	5	Sergeant Hans Bowski
6	Corporal Heinrich Haase	5	Lieutenant von Breiten Landenberg
6	Lieutenant Colonel Erich Hahn	5	Captain Frederich Burchhardt
6	Lieutenant Georg Hengl	5	Lieutenant August Burkard
6	Lieutenant Heinrich Henkel	5	Lieutenant Karl Christ
6	Lieutenant Albert Hets	5	Lieutenant Colonel Theodor Croneiss
6	Lieutenant Robert Hildebrandt		
6	Sergeant Josef Hohlg	5	Lieutenant August Delling
6	Lieutenant Otto Höhne	5	Lieutenant Willi Fahlbusch
6	Corporal Michael Hutterer	5	Sergeant Gaim
6	Lieutenant Hans Imelmann	5	Lieutenant Sylvester Garsztka
6	Lieutenant Johannes Jensen	5	Lieutenant Johannes Gildmeister
6	Lieutenant Erich Just	5	Lieutenant Siegfried Gussmann
6	Sergeant Gustav Klaudat	5	Lieutenant Kurt Haber
6	Lieutenant Erich Koenig	5	Lieutenant August Hano
6	Sergeant Hans Körner	5	Lieutenant Kurt Hetze
6	Sergeant Fritz Krebs	5	Sergeant Fritz Jakobsen
6	Lieutenant Hermann Kunz	5	Sergeant Hermann Juhnke
6	Lieutenant Alfred Lenz	5	Lieutenant Werner Junck
6	Lieutenant Ludwig Luer	5	Sergeant Otto Klaiber
6	Lieutenant Friedrich Mallinckrodt	5	Lieutenant Wilhelm Kohlbach
		5	Corporal Johann Kopka
6	Lieutenant Colonel Hans Mettlich	5	Lieutenant Kurt Küppers
		5	Lieutenant Wilhelm Leusch
6	Lieutenant Alfred Mohr	5	Lieutenant Colonel Heinrich Lorenz
6	Lieutenant Hans Oberländer		
6	Lieutenant Arthur Rahn	5	Corporal Hans Marwede
6	Lieutenant Rudolf Rienau	5	Corporal Erich Meyer
6	Lieutenant Karl Schmückle	5	Lieutenant Werner Niethammer
6	Lieutenant Gunther Schüster	5	Lieutenant Hans von der Osten
6	Lieutenant Willi Schulz	5	Lieutenant Rudolf Otto
6	Lieutenant Heinrich Seywald	5	Corporal Leopold Reimann
6	Corporal Erich Sonneck	5	Lieutenant Hans Rosencratz
6	Lieutenant Otto Splitgerber	5	Sergeant Paul Rothe
6	Lieutenant Rudolf Stark	5	Sergeant Richard Rübe
6	Sergeant Georg Staudacher	5	Lieutenant Theodor Rumpel
6	Corporal Karl Treiber	5	Lieutenant Alfons Scheicher
6	Sergeant Reinhard Treptow	5	Corporal Johann Schlimpen
6	Sergeant Kurt Ungewitter	5	Lieutenant Roman Schneider
6	Lieutenant Colonel Hans Waldhausen	5	Lieutenant Herbert Schröder
		5	Sergeant Friedrich Schumacher
5	Lieutenant Hans Auer	5	Sergeant Erich Schütze
5	Lieutenant Joachim von Bertrab	5	Lieutenant Conrad Schwartz
5	Corporal Rudolf Besel	5	Lieutenant Eugen Simpelkamp
5	Lieutenant Colonel Heinrich von Boddien	5	Lieutenant Wilhelm Sommer
		5	Sergeant Wilhelm Stöhr
5	Lieutenant Herbert Bog	5	Sergeant Karl Strünkelnberg

Score	Rank and Name	Score	Rank and Name
5	Lieutenant Colonel Kurt Student	5	Lieutenant Hans Viebig
5	Lieutenant Alwin Thurm	5	Sergeant Ernst Wiehle
5	Sergeant Oswald Tränkner	5	Lieutenant Ernst Wiessner
5	Lieutenant Gerold Tschentschel	5	Lieutenant Kurt Wisseman
5	Lieutenant Alfred Ulmer	5	Captain Martin Zander
5	Lieutenant Hermann Vallendor		

Technical Data World War I Aircraft

GREAT BRITAIN

Aircraft	Crew	Engine	Wing span	Fuselage length	Loaded weight	Performance at altitude	Service ceiling
AIRCO (DE HAVILLAND)							
D.H.2	1	110 Le Rhone	28′ 3″	25′ 2″	1,547	85/5,000	14,500
D.H.4	2	250 Rolls-Royce	42′ 8″	30′ 8″	3,313	119/3,000	16,000
D.H.5	1	110 Le Rhone	25′ 8″	22′	1,492	102/10,000	15,500
D.H.9a	2	230 Siddeley	42′ 5″	30′ 6″	3,669	111/10,000	15,500
ARMSTRONG WHITWORTH							
F.K.8	2	160 Beardmore	43′ 4″	31′ 5″	2,811	95/6,500	13,000
BRISTOL							
Scout	1	80 Gnome	24′ 7″	20′ 8″	1,190	84/5,000	15,500
F.2b Fighter	2	280 Rolls-Royce	39′ 3″	25′ 10″	2,590	113/10,000	20,000
HANDLEY PAGE							
V/400	4	2 275 Rolls-Royce	100′	62′ 10″	14,022	85/5,000	8,500
V/1500	5–7	4 375 Rolls-Royce	126′	64′	30,000	90/6,000	11,000
A. V. ROE							
504	2	130 Le Rhone	36′	29′ 5″	1,829	85/10,000	16,000
ROYAL AIRCRAFT FACTORY							
B.E.2a	2	70 Renault	38′ 7″	29′ 6″	1,600	72	9,500
B.E.2c	2	90 R.A.F.	37′	27′ 3″	2,142	72/6,500	10,000
B.E.2e	2	90 R.A.F.	40′ 9″	27′ 3″	2,100	82/6,500	10,000
B.E.12	2	150 R.A.F.	37′	27′ 3″	2,352	97/6,500	12,500
R.E.5	2	120 Beardmore	44′ 6″	26′ 2″	N.A.	78	N.A.
R.E.7	2	150 R.A.F.	57′	31′ 10″	3,449	85	6,500
R.E.8	2	150 R.A.F.	42′ 7″	27′ 10″	2,678	95	13,000
S.E.2	1	80 Gnome	27′ 6″	20′ 6″	1,120	85	N.A.
S.E.5a	1	200 Hispano-Suiza	26′ 8″	20′ 11″	2,000	132/6,500	19,500

Aircraft	Crew	Engine	Wing span	Fuselage length	Loaded weight	Performance at altitude	Service ceiling
SOPWITH							
Tabloid	1	80 Gnome	25′ 6″	20′ 4″	1,120	92	N.A.
Baby	1	110 Clerget	25′ 8″	23′	1,715	100	N.A.
Pup	1	80 Le Rhone	26′ 6″	19′ 4″	1,225	103/9,000	17,500
1½-Strutter	2	110 Clerget	33′ 6″	25′ 3″	2,149	92/12,000	13,000
Triplane	1	110 Clerget	26′ 6″	18′ 10″	1,541	117/5,000	20,500
F.1 Camel	1	130 Clerget	28′	18′ 9″	1,453	124/6,500	19,000
2F.1	1	150 Bentley	26′ 11″	18′ 8″	1,530	124/6,500	17,300
5F.1 Dolphin	1	200 Hispano-Suiza	32′ 6″	22′ 3″	1,911	131	21,000
7F.1 Snipe	1	230 Bentley	30′ 1″	19′ 9″	2,020	121/10,000	20,000
VICKERS							
F.B.5 Gun Bus	2	100 Gnome	36′ 6″	27′ 2″	2,050	70/5,000	9,000
F.B.9	2	100 Gnome	33′ 9″	28′ 5″	1,892	80/5,000	11,000
F.B.12	2	100 Gnome	26′	21′ 6″	1,400	93/5,000	14,000

FRANCE

Aircraft	Crew	Engine	Wing span	Fuselage length	Loaded weight	Performance at altitude	Service ceiling
BLÉRIOT							
XI	1	70 Gnome	33' 11"	27' 11"	1,290	66	N.A.
BREGUET							
14	2	300 Renault	47' 3"	29' 7"	3,380	110/6,500	19,000
CAUDRON							
G.3	2	100 Anzani	43' 5"	22' 6"	1,619	70	10,000
G.4	2	2 80 Le Rhone	55' 5"	23' 6"	2,970	82/6,500	14,000
R.11	3	2 220 Hispano-Suiza	58' 9"	36' 11"	4,773	113/6,500	19,500
FARMAN							
S.7	2	80 Gnome	51'	37' 3"	1,887	59	N.A.
S.11	2	70 Renault	53'	30' 8"	2,046	66	N.A.
F.20	2	80 Gnome	44' 9"	26' 6"	1,440	60	N.A.
F.40	2	160 Renault	57' 9"	30' 4"	2,469	94/6,500	13,100
HANROIT							
HD-1	1	130 Le Rhone	28' 6"	19' 2"	1,350	116	23,600
MORANE-SAULNIER							
A-1	1	160 Gnome	27' 10"	18' 6"	1,425	129/6,500	23,000
L	1	80 Gnome	33' 9"	20' 9"	1,396	71	12,000
N	1	100 Le Rhone	27' 3"	22'	1,122	102/6,500	13,000
NIEUPORT							
10	2	80 Gnome	25' 11"	22' 11"	1,452	87	N.A.
11	1	80 Gnome	24' 6"	19'	1,210	97	15,000
12	2	100 Clerget	29' 7"	23' 6"	1,155	98	N.A.
16	1	110 Le Rhone	24' 6"	19'	1,133	103/6,500	N.A.
17	1	110 Le Rhone	27' 3"	19' 6"	1,233	107/6,500	17,400
28	1	160 Gnome	26' 9"	21' 2"	1,540	128	20,000

Aircraft	Crew	Engine	Wing span	Fuselage length	Loaded weight	Performance at altitude	Service ceiling
SALMSON							
2A.2	2	260 Salmson	38' 8"	27' 11"	2,954	115/6,560	20,500
S.P.A.D.							
S-7	1	180 Hispano-Suiza	25' 6"	20' 1"	1,100	119/6,500	18,000
S-13	1	200 Hispano-Suiza	26' 4"	20' 8"	1,815	130/6,500	22,300
VOISIN							
5	2	150 Salmson	48' 5"	31' 3"	2,513	62	11,500
8	2	220 Peugeot	61' 8"	36' 2"	4,103	75/6,500	14,000

GERMANY

Aircraft	Crew	Engine	Wing span	Fuselage length	Loaded weight	Performance at altitude	Service ceiling
ALLGEMEINE ELEKTRIZITATS GESELLSCHAFT (A.E.G.)							
C-4	2	160 Mercedes	22' 2"	23' 5"	2,469	98	16,400
G-4	3	2 260 Mercedes	60' 4"	32' 4"	8,000	91/4,920	14,760
ALBATROS							
B-2	2	100 Mercedes	42'	25'	2,372	66	9,840
C-1	2	160 Mercedes	42' 4"	25' 9"	2,618	87	9,840
C-3	2	150 Benz	38' 4"	26' 3"	2,983	87	11,150
C-5	2	220 Mercedes	41' 11"	29' 4"	2,352	106	N.A.
C-11	2	260 Mercedes	47' 2"	29'	3,606	109	N.A.
D-1	1	150 Benz	28' 4"	24' 4"	1,976	109	17,000
D-3	1	160 Mercedes	29' 7"	24'	1,949	115	18,000
D-5	1	180 Mercedes	29' 7"	24'	2,013	117/3,280	20,500
D-11	1	160 Siemens-Halske	26' 3"	18' 3"	1,591	118	26,000
AVIATIK							
C-1	2	160 Mercedes	41'	26'	2,732	89	11,480
C-3	2	200 Benz	43' 7"	25' 10"	3,146	97	16,400
DEUTSCHE FLUGZEUG-WERKE (D.F.W.)							
B-1	2	100 Mercedes	45' 11"	27' 7"	2,238	75	9,840
C-5	2	200 Benz	43' 6"	25' 10"	3,146	96	20,990
DORNIER							
D-1	1	185 B.M.W.	25' 8"	20' 1"	1,914	125	26,500
FOKKER							
E-1	1	80 Oberursel	28'	22' 2"	1,239	82	10,000
E-2	1	100 Oberursel	32' 8"	23' 2"	1,340	87	12,000
E-4	1	160 Oberursel	32' 1"	24' 8"	1,593	100	13,500
D-1	1	120 Mercedes	29' 8"	18' 10"	1,476	93	13,100
D-2	1	100 Oberursel	28' 8"	20' 11"	1,267	94	13,100

Aircraft	Crew	Engine	Wing span	Fuselage length	Loaded weight	Performance at altitude	Service ceiling
D-5	1	100 Oberursel	28′ 3″	19′ 10″	1,245	106	13,000
D-6	1	100 Oberursel	25′ 1″	20′ 5″	1,283	125	19,500
D-7	1	160 Mercedes	29′ 3″	22′ 9″	1,936	116/3,280	19,600
D-8	1	110 Oberursel	27′ 4″	19′ 3″	1,334	127	21,000
Dr.1	1	110 Oberursel	23′ 7″	18′ 11″	1,289	115	19,600
FRIEDRICHSHAFEN							
G-3	3	2 260 Mercedes	77′ 9″	42′ 1″	8,686	88	14,765
GOTHA							
G-5	3	2 260 Mercedes	77′ 9″	40′ 6″	8,763	87/12,000	21,325
HALBERSTADT							
CL-2	2	160 Mercedes	35′ 4″	23′ 11″	2,493	103	13,500
CL-4	2	160 Mercedes	35′ 3″	21′ 5″	2,349	103	16,400
C-5	2	220 Benz	44′ 8″	22′ 8″	2,730	106	16,400
D-2	1	120 Mercedes	28′ 10″	23′ 11″	1,606	90	9,840
HANNOVER							
CL-2	2	180 Argus	39′ 4″	25′ 5″	2,442	96	24,600
CL-3	2	160 Mercedes	38′ 4″	24′ 10″	2,365	102/2,000	24,600
LUFTVERKEHRS GESELLSCHAFT (L.V.G. ROLAND)							
C-2	2	160 Mercedes	33′ 8″	25′ 3″	2,825	103	13,120
D-2	1	160 Mercedes	29′ 3″	22′ 9″	1,749	105	13,100
D-6	1	150 Benz	30′ 10″	20′ 9″	1,892	114	19,680
PFALZ							
D-3A	1	180 Mercedes	30′ 8″	24′ 10″	2,057	112/2,000	17,000
D-12	1	160 Mercedes	29′ 6″	20′ 11″	1,973	115	18,500
E-1	1	80 Oberursel	36′ 8″	22′ 6″	1,705	90	10,000

Aircraft	Crew	Engine	Wing span	Fuselage length	Loaded weight	Performance at altitude	Service ceiling
RUMPLER							
Taube	1	110 Mercedes	48' 6"	33' 6"	1,761	55	N.A.
C-1	2	160 Mercedes	39' 10"	25' 9"	2,932	94	16,570
C-4	2	260 Mercedes	41' 6"	27' 7"	3,366	106/3,280	20,990
C-7	2	240 Maybach	41' 2"	26' 11"	3,267	109/6,560	23,945
SIEMENS-SCHUCKERT							
D-1	1	110 Siemens-Halske	24' 7"	19' 8"	1,485	97/3,280	N.A.
D-3	1	160 Siemens-Halske	27' 7"	18' 8"	1,584	112	26,500
D-4	1	200 Siemens-Halske	27' 5"	18' 8"	1,620	118	21,100
ZEPPELIN							
R-6	7	4 260 Mercedes	.38' 5"	72' 6"	26,066	84	14,170

Index